PRAISE FOR

French Accents

"Anita's French style is both inspirational and aspirational. She has a distinctly personal—and approachable—way of combining the rustic with the refined. *French Accents* should be a go-to design resource for [adding] a bit of French style to your home."

—Donna Talley, regional editor, producer and photo stylist,
Better Homes & Gardens

"I love how down-to-earth Anita is in her approach to French decorating, which so many women would like to emulate. With *French Accents*, she takes the idea of it being unattainable for normal folks with real budgets out of the picture and shares easy ways to add French touches in a fresh, simple, modern way."

—Rhoda Vickers, lifestyle blogger,
author of the Southern Hospitality *blog*

"Anita Joyce has the most charming way to instill French accents into interiors. In *French Accents*, she shares her experiences, knowledge, and tips for incorporating the many iconic elements that define a French interior, [including] showcasing architectural details, . . . choosing a flattering color palate, uniting well-aged furnishings with elegant ones, or spot-lighting textures and finishes, to name a few.

"With an easy-to-follow plan, how-to list, and well-chosen examples, Anita takes you on a candid and informative step-by-step journey to achieve the much-loved look.

"Though your home might be far from the storied buildings of Paris, the cobblestone streets of the French countryside, or the lavender fields of Provence, *French Accents* gently demonstrates how to easily and effortlessly infuse character and right touches with confidence to any space, may it be in a farmhouse, a city home, a cottage, or a chateau.

"*French Accents* is a tribute to the essential and uncontrived mix of flair and function that epitomizes French style and *joie de vivre*."

—Fifi O'Neill, author of several books (including Prairie-Style Weddings:
Rustic and Romantic Farm, Woodland, and Garden Celebrations*)*
and editor of French Country Style *and* Tuscan Home *magazines*

"The term *French decorating* used to somewhat intimidate me. Let's face it, when you yourself decorate with pallet wood, anything else sounds pretty upscale! Anita's approach changed all that. When I glanced through the pages of her inspiring book, one word came to mind: *Comfort*. You will find something in every single room you will fall in love with . . . no matter what you call your own style!

"Thanks for breaking that barrier down for me, Anita. I am a new French decorating fan!"

—*Donna Williams, founder of* Funky Junk Interiors
and author of the Funky Junk *blog*

"Anita is a master when it comes to creating beautiful, livable French-style spaces. Yes, this book is overflowing with inspirational images to spark with your creativity. More than that, though, Anita's casual approach and friendly words make re-creating this style accessible."

—*Marian Parsons, founder of* Mustard Seed Interiors
and author of the Miss Mustard Seed *blog*

"Opening Anita's beautiful book is like stepping into France at its ethereal best! Immediately struck by breathtaking Parisian images, you know you are in for a very special treat! The pages transport the reader into the fascinating world of French decor and old-world charm.

"Do not let the sublime images of French decor fool you. The book is down-to-earth practical and offers the reader an easy-to-follow system of getting an authentic French look. Anita spares no details as she takes us step-by-step from learning about French style to the finishing touches of several beautiful French-inspired rooms and do-it-yourself projects. *French Accents* is a storybook of one homemaker's love of all things French and her decorating journey as well as a savvy workbook to learn from and discover the art of French decorating.

"A true delight for Francophile decorators and the novice as well!"

—*Yvonne Pratt, author of the* StoneGable *blog*

"I have been a fan of Anita's style and flair for French decorating for years. One of the incredible things about Anita is her ability to elevate even the most ordinary of things into something truly extraordinary with the true eye of a designer. She has inspired me and so many others with her creativity and photography and her beautiful French country decor. This incredible book captures the essence of Anita's style, grace, and humor and inspires all of us to introduce a little something amazing in our own little corner of the world. Well done, my friend!"

—*KariAnne Wood, founder of* Thistlewood Farms
and author of the Thistlewood Farms *blog*

FRENCH ACCENTS

FARMHOUSE FRENCH STYLE
FOR TODAY'S HOME

SECOND EDITION

FRENCH ACCENTS

FARMHOUSE FRENCH STYLE FOR TODAY'S HOME

SECOND EDITION

Anita Joyce

AUTHOR OF THE POPULAR BLOG *CEDAR HILL FARMHOUSE*

Plain Sight Publishing | An Imprint of Cedar Fort, Inc. | Springville, Utah

ISBN 13: 978-1-4621-2228-8

Published by Plain Sight Publishing, an imprint of Cedar Fort, Inc.
2373 W. 700 S., Springville, UT 84663
Distributed by Cedar Fort, Inc., www.cedarfort.com

THE LIBRARY OF CONGRESS HAS CATALOGED THE EARLIER EDITION AS FOLLOWS:

Joyce, Anita, 1961- author.
 French accents / Anita Joyce.
 pages cm
 ISBN 978-1-4621-1678-2 (alk. paper)
 1. Interior decoration. I. Title.

NK2115.J77 2015
747—dc23

2015007613

Cover and page design by Lauren Error and M. Shaun McMurdie
Cover design © 2018 Cedar Fort, Inc.
Edited by Jessica Romrell and Kaitlin Barwick
Photography by Anita Joyce

Printed in Korea

10 9 8 7 6 5 4 3 2 1

Printed on acid-free paper

To Kevin, for seeing me not as who I am but who I strive to be.
To Elise, for showing me how to dance with the angels. And to Evie,
for reminding me that life is an adventure.

CONTENTS

ACKNOWLEDGMENTS

I really want to thank my family for supporting me through the years with the blog, the podcast, and now this book. Thank you Kevin, Evangeline, and Elise. Miss Haydee Cortez kept the home fires burning, while Evie Joyce, Evie Sweeten, Kelli Hays, and Lois Christensen helped keep my blog running. I also want to thank Rit Johnson and Brandon Kinsey with Ridgewater Homes, Inc. for building my dream home.

I began blogging because my friend Peggy Born believed in me. She read my blog, even when no one else did. Of course none of this would have been possible without the Lord, through whom all blessings flow. I also want to thank my readers, who are generous and caring. My blogger friends have also been supportive and gracious. I appreciate all of them and feel I'm a better person, writer, and photographer because of them

I also want to thank my girls, Yvonne Pratt and Kelly Wilkniss, my cohosts from our podcast, "Decorating Tips and Tricks." They have been a constant source of support through the tumultuous ups and downs of our business.

Introduction

Long ago, during a difficult time in my life, I found myself mired in a pool of self-pity, wondering if there was more to life. Desperate for a diversion, I attended an antique auction on a whim, not knowing what to expect. The next thing I knew, I was on my way home with a handsome tall French stranger. He, or more correctly, "it" was actually an eight-foot-tall antique French armoire. Still . . . I was in love! I could hardly contain my excitement as my eyes gently traced the intricate carving along the top of the piece. I marveled at the carved details, the arched door, hand-made dovetail joints, and its age (over 150 years old). My mind wandered as I dreamed of who must have owned it and what their lives were like. Where did they live? Were their lives as romantic as I imagined?

I couldn't get the first French owners out of my head. More and more during the day, my thoughts turned to my armoire's previous life in France. I was drawn there in a magnetic way I couldn't explain. When I confided my growing obsession of all things French to my mother, she informed me of my French ancestry. I hadn't known about it before,

because the family name had been changed to an anglicized version over 200 years ago.

Discovering my French roots not only legitimized my fascination with France but also made me even more determined to visit, even though I knew very little about France and spoke no French. In my mind's eye, I was there, basking in the sunshine amidst a field of lavender, reading under the shade of a large gnarly tree, or walking down a lovely boulevard in Paris to a nearby patisserie for a *café au lait* and croissant.

Soon enough, I convinced my husband to take a French vacation. Actually it wasn't that difficult. After a brief stay in Paris, we were off to the south of France. As we arrived in the Luberon Valley, I quickly declared it to be the most stunning place I had ever been. The little dreamy town, high on a hill, looked much as it did 200 years before, with its cobbled streets and stone houses. Pots of gardenias lined the boulevard in front of the homes, while in the distance I could see laundry sparkling in the sun as it hung on the clothesline.

Each morning I would throw open the old wooden shutters to reveal the glorious valley below.

As the sun's rays streamed in, it felt as if heaven itself had invaded the room. Birds sung in the distance, and I could hear the soft sounds of the village coming to life. Glasses clanked at the outdoor café nearby as the waiters prepared for breakfast. Neighbors greeted each other as they picked up their morning paper and opened their windows for the day. I loved everything about life here, not just the furniture. People seemed happy, they enjoyed life, savored meals, and spent time outdoors.

I remember thinking it must be the most glorious place on earth. Here, I felt safe and isolated from the harsh outside world. I wanted to bottle it all up and take it home with me, and then a thought formed: Why not? Was it possible to live a French life back home? The seed was planted; the dream was born. I left home restless and unfocused, I returned with a passion and a mission. I wanted to live my life in the French way surrounded by beauty, savoring time with my family and friends. And so I began the journey to create a home with laid-back French style.

This book is about the journey to create Farmhouse French style in a comfortable, inviting way that welcomes friends and family while making them feel celebrated and loved. It's about adding French accents to your home, combining cozy, rustic charm with a quiet, elegant style. It also includes DIY tips and tricks so you can do it all on a budget.

CHAPTER 1: IS IT FRENCH?

Upon returning from my first trip to France, I found myself smitten with French decor. I was determined to convert my very plain, very '70's suburban American home into a country French retreat. There was only one catch—well, three, to be exact.

1. I only had one French item in my entire home.

2. I was on a tight budget.

3. I had no clue what exactly constituted French design.

A "sane" person, or one with above average intelligence, might have given up at that point, but not me. I was a woman on a mission. Telling me not to convert my home to French décor was like telling a fish not to swim. I knew it would happen, I just didn't know how I was going to get from point A to point B. I have found that a determination to do a certain thing is more important than the knowledge required to accomplish the thing. Sure, I didn't know what I was doing, but I wasn't going to let that get in my way. I wanted to give my home French accents, but I hadn't a clue how to do it. I looked at what I did know. I could look at a piece of furniture and tell if it was French or not. That seemed like a no-brainer.

I even found some inexpensive sources for French furniture; it was the rest of the stuff—the bedding, curtains, lamps, and accessories—that was the issue. How would I be able to look at a lamp, for example, and know whether it was French or not? What about a candlestick? I started with what I knew was French—fleur-de-lis, roosters, toile fabric, and of course, the Eiffel Tower. I decided that roosters would make my home look French. And so I began to buy up every ceramic rooster within a 50-mile radius. My house began to resemble a chicken farm, without the smell. In fact, one day a male friend was visiting and he asked if I had attended the University of South Carolina. I found the question very odd indeed, and asked why on earth he would ask such a question. "The roosters," he said. "Their mascot is a rooster, or more precisely, they are the fighting gamecocks." Inside I was a horrified that he didn't "get it," but on the outside I smiled as if he were the most clever guest we had ever entertained. Then, I began to wonder if my country French look was really working for me.

(It wasn't.) I tried to reassure myself. I mean really, he didn't know the first thing about design. I began to picture him living in a trailer park sitting in his underwear with a can of beer. Of course he was a nice man, but that day, I didn't like him very much. Couldn't he tell that this was first-class French design here? The nerve!

I began to rethink my whole "roosters + fleur-de-lis + toile + mini Eiffel towers = country French design." I realized it was time to do a bit more research. I decided I would work for a furniture and accessory store that specialized in country French décor. I worked there for 5 years, spent every penny I made on furniture, and soaked up every bit of French design I could. I read magazines and books on French design. There weren't many décor blogs at the time, so I wasn't reading them . . . yet.

One day, I found some new plates at a discount store. They were charming little salad plates in a soft blue, and they had a basket weave design. I thought they were charming and turned them over as I always do to see where they were made. "Made in France," said the stamp on the back. I hugged them to my bosom and did a happy dance in the aisle. I had the real deal here. No matter what the plates looked like, they were French. Now I had real French dishes. And then I realized that if I hadn't turned them over, I would not have known they were made in France, so now I was even more confused about what constituted French décor.

So how can you tell whether a basket, for example, is French or not French? What if it isn't made in France? Does it actually have to be made in France to give a room that French look? These were questions that I asked myself, and I began to form my own opinions on the subject. When looking at a country French room, it looked very similar to an English country room to me, with a few exceptions—more curves and flourishes, more extravagances.

I have not studied French design at some fancy school, or really any school for that matter. The thoughts presented in this book are my take on French design based on my travel to France, working many years in that quaint furniture store, and writing about French design on my blog: www.cedarhillfarmhouse.com.

And here is what I have found: To create a French look in your home, you do not need to spend a fortune. You do not need to throw everything out that isn't French. You probably have many elements in your home that work in country French design. My take is that if the item is consistent with country French design, and you like it, then keep it. French design is a broad category and has a lot of overlap with English and American design. For those wanting to create country French design in their home, my suggestion if you are on a tight budget is to do a bit at a time and to gradually move your home in the French direction.

Common Myths

I think there are a lot of misconceptions about French design. Not only are people confused about what constitutes French design, but there are some wrong ideas floating around that I would like to debunk:

Myth 1: *French furniture is not affordable.*

The truth: Obviously, some French furniture is very expensive. It has an eternal appeal, which means prices don't often go down. I have always said that if you put an English chair next to a comparable French chair, all other things being equal, the French one is always going to cost more. All of that is true; however, French furniture can still be found for reasonable prices, and in some cases, it can be found for a bargain. When I was a kid, there was a popular saying, "It's all in the wrist." When young boys would be wowed by some super athlete and they would ask him how he did it, he would say, "Well boys, it's all in the wrist." This would leave the boys with no clue how to do it for themselves, and it somehow made it not sound easier but more elusive. For me, buying French furniture at bargain prices isn't in the wrist, but it is in knowing where to shop. The same chair for example might sell for one place at $150 and $1500 at another. I'll give you the pros and cons on shopping different places.

Myth 2: *You have to do an entire room in French style for it to look good.*

The truth: There are lots of different French styles. On one end of the spectrum, there are those rooms that are quintessentially French, with layer upon layer of French details, and on the other end, rooms with just one French chair. The odd thing is that I've seen both work well. French is a style that transcends time. It works with many different styles, from contemporary to

country French. I'm sure there are exceptions to this rule, but most rooms look even better with French accents, even if the room itself isn't actually French. The other thing I have noticed is that French style is so distinctive that even if you just have a few French pieces in a room, visitors remember the room as being French. I remember when I first began collecting French furniture. I only had two French pieces in my entire house; they were two French armoires. Even then, friends referred to my style as French.

Myth 3: *French design is too formal for modern life.*

The truth: As with many myths, there is some truth in this one. Formal French design like what you might see at Versailles is the height of formality and fussiness. Decorating a room as it would have been decorated for eighteenth-century French court is far too formal and impractical for today's living. But a French chair here and there, along with other French accents and touches, adds a bit of finesse to a room. On the other end of the spectrum, Country French style—the style

typically seen in country homes—has always been relaxed and easy. I think my approach to French design is very simple, and fits well with modern life. I shy away from too much fluff and frills. I've worked to update my version of French design so that it is cleaner and simpler. It just works better for my modern lifestyle.

The bottom line is that you CAN do French design on a budget to fit your current lifestyle, without throwing out all of your current furniture. I would also like to add that it won't take you a lifetime to figure it out, because by the time you are done reading this book, you'll have several ideas on how to do it. Let's get started!

CHAPTER 2: START HERE

A beautiful room is not just a room filled with beautiful things. The beauty comes from how the individual pieces work together to create a room whose sum is equal to more than its parts. Consider this: the thing that makes a song melodious and memorable is not the specific notes that are used, but how the composer/songwriter weaves the words and the melody together. Sure, you need to use quality materials to make a beautiful room, but it is how everything works together than makes a beautiful room "sing." A sofa that feels harmonious in one room can feel like nails on a chalkboard in another, so you'll need to put some focus into studying how your pieces work together.

Good design means the room flows, it has balance, it draws you in, and says, "stay . . ." A beautiful room is one that comes together—a room that feels complete. It should feel like it has balance and flow. It needs some symmetry—but also some asymmetry. It needs varying heights and textures, fabrics that work together and don't fight. The most difficult part of interior decorating, in my opinion, is making it all work together. Since I am self-taught, when I work on a room, I am not thinking through steps taught in an interior design class. I am simply doing what comes naturally to me, without considering any formulas or design principles. It is like walking. I don't think about all that goes into walking from the car to the front door, it's just a part of life.

Having said that, I have made an attempt to document my process, so I could share it with you. As I made an effort to think through how I approach a room, I realized I do have a process that I follow, more or less. I just wasn't aware of it, until I sat down and thought about it. In this chapter, I'll outline the basic steps I go through, and in Chapter 20, I'll walk you through how I transformed rooms at our farm, from start to finish.

I know based on the emails I receive, that decorating does not come naturally to a lot of people. The focus here is on the "how to." It is one thing to pick out a beautiful chair, but making an entire room harmonious and beautiful is a different skill set. So where do you begin? At the beginning, of course! I like to start at my front door and walk into my house as a guest might on a home tour. I pretend it is the first time I have seen the house and try to take everything in as a visitor would. I begin to notice things I had ignored before, like the dust bunnies in the corner and the dead plant, oh dear . . .

I ask myself questions.

Does the room feel warm and inviting?

Do things flow?

Are there places where one design stops abruptly and another starts?

I go through my house and make a note of everything that doesn't look "right" to me. If it is simply a matter of removing something, I can do that right away. If we are talking about replacing a kitchen table, then obviously I can't take the old one out until I have a replacement table.

STEP 1: Take notes, listing the things you don't like about each room.

As you enter a room, take a fresh look at the room and try to see it with fresh eyes. Here are some questions to ask yourself about each room. Let these questions be a starting point. You can add your own and take out the ones that don't make sense in your situation.

STEP 2: Photograph the room.

Photographing the room helps you determine how your room looks in an unbiased way. There are problems that are difficult to see unless the room is photographed. Sometimes the room seems fine in person, but when you photograph it, you realize the wall color is too strong, or a chair is too big for the space. This is something DIY bloggers know. I thought the green walls in my daughter's bedroom were dated looking, but still looked okay. I mean, it didn't look that bad. At least, that's what I told myself. When I took a photo to use on my blog, the photo told a different story. The room looked terrible to me! I might be able to lie to myself while walking in the room, but seeing it in a photo is another story. It's like when I think I look great, then I see a photo of myself and realize I need to lose 5 pounds. (Okay maybe 10.) Photos don't lie. They show you things you can often overlook in person.

QUESTIONS TO ASK YOURSELF

1. What is the first thing you notice about the room?

2. What feeling does it evoke?

3. Does it feel warm and inviting?

4. Is this a room you enjoy being in?

5. Does it feel dated?

6. What do you like about the room?

7. What would you like to change about the room?

8. Do you like the colors in the room?

9. Does the room feel cluttered?

10. List the items that you don't like here.

11. List the items that you *do* like here.

12. Does the room flow, or does it feel choppy?

13. Does it feel balanced?

14. Do the colors and patterns work together or feel like they are fighting?

15. Is the furniture functional for the room?

16. Is the furniture layout working for the room?

STEP 3: Review decorating guidelines.

Read the chapter on Decorating Guidelines (see pages 25–44) and use those guidelines as you assess your room. These guidelines are generic guidelines not specific to Farmhouse French style; however, they are important things to keep in mind. I chose to include these guidelines, even though they are generic, because I believe these guidelines will help you when decorating your home. Be sure to make notes as you go through the list.

STEP 4: Review the Farmhouse French List.

The Farmhouse French list gives you a list of specific things you can add to a room to give it Farmhouse French accents. You don't need to incorporate all of the ideas, but these are easy ways to give your home a French feel. Make notes on which items you plan to add to your room.

STEP 5: Focus on one room at a time.

In general, I try to focus on one room at a time. The reason I do one room at a time is that it is very satisfying to complete a room. It is not satisfying to have five rooms partially done. I like checking things off my list; I feel I have accomplished something. The other reason I like to take it room by room is because it is less stressful and easier to do. Keeping track of what is going on in one room is far easier than keeping track of three or four. Some days I can barely remember if I combed my hair, so my one-room-at-a-time approach makes my life more manageable. Working for a long time and not having one room actually finished can be very demoralizing. There are some exceptions to my "one room at a time" approach. Sometimes you have a big project in a room and no funds or time to work on it right away. I usually shelve those projects until my schedule opens up or I have the funds for the project.

Another aspect of my strategy is to decide whether to focus on the easiest room or the one that is most important to me. But here is a tip: I keep the list of things I am

looking for on my phone. I shop a lot at second-hand stores and consignment stores. You bargain shoppers know how this works. Sometimes I see exactly what I want for a room, but that is not the room I am currently working on. If I really like it, and the price is really good, I go ahead and buy it, even if I am not "officially" working on that room yet, since the item would be gone if I waited to make the purchase. Similarly, if I have painting projects lined up for several rooms, I often do them all at once. Painting is such a mess that I try to paint everything that needs painting while the drop cloths, paint brushes, and so forth are all out and I still have my painting clothes on. Ditto on sewing. When I get my sewing machine out, I get on a roll and pop out the cushions, pillows, curtains, slipcovers, or whatever I am working on all at once.

Your decorating plan should include all proposed changes to the room. They might include

1. Furniture placement
2. Buying list
3. Electrical projects like light fixtures
4. Sewing projects
5. Upholstery work
6. Paint projects
7. Plumbing projects, like a new sink or faucet
8. New flooring
9. Fabrics to be used
10. Furniture to be purchased
11. Tablecloths or other linens
12. Silverware
13. Dishes
14. Baskets
15. Artwork or mirrors
16. Enamelware
17. Crates
18. Clocks
19. Lamps
20. Bedding
21. Accessories
22. Pillows and throws

STEP 6: Develop a decorating plan.

This is one of the more difficult parts of decorating. It is often easy to see what is wrong with a room, but what should you do to fix the room? The difficult part comes in deciding how to make the room shine. Sometimes the answer is as simple as a rearranging the furniture, while other times, major pieces of furniture need to be replaced.

After you complete your decorating plan, you should have a list of things that you need to buy and a project list. Some things you might be planning to buy right away, while other things may not happen for a few years. I try to not only make a note of what I want to purchase but also a time frame, even if it just says "short term" or "long term." Keep in mind that some things probably won't work according to plan. Be flexible. A chair you bought for one room might look better in another. A rug you bought might need to be returned. Some things may not be returnable, so you will need to figure out what you will do if something doesn't work. That is another reason to have similar design for all of the rooms in your house. If something you bought doesn't work in one room, maybe it will work in another. The "Plan B" is especially important when you shop at thrift stores, where returns aren't always accepted.

STEP 7: Complete the decorating work.

Here, you follow through with your decorating plan. Sometimes it can be completed in a day, while other times, if the work to be done is extensive and the budget is limited, it could literally take years. Don't stress if things in the room don't work—just pull out what isn't working, and try something else.

STEP 8: Review changes and tweak as needed.

I suggest you take more photos and review them. Tweak the room as necessary. If you don't like something or something doesn't seem quite right, try moving things around. Take things out, move things in from another room, or try exchanging the item that doesn't work. Remember, mistakes are okay, and they are part of the learning process. As I tell my daughter all the time, everyone has failures. The difference between a loser and a winner is that a loser gives up after a failure, while a winner keeps going.

CHAPTER 3: DECORATING GUIDELINES

Even if you can't articulate your guidelines for decorating, I suspect you have some. It is like writing a sentence. There are millions of different sentences you can write, but still you need to be sure that your subject and verb agree. If you are a native English speaker, then when you speak English, you probably don't think about if your subject agrees with your verb, you just speak. You are not even tempted to say "She walk" or "They walks." It is the same with decorating; there are many things that decorators may not think about that they just do automatically. For someone who speaks English as a second language, it's very different. One must then learn how to speak properly to say things correctly and in a way that people can comprehend.

Before I started this book, I honestly never thought through what I was doing, I just did it. I experiment, I make mistakes, I try new things. It can be a messy process, but I feel like the real proof is in the end result. In an effort to explain my design process, I made an effort to walk through it so I could capture it in words and share it with you, not unlike how you explain to a friend how to get to your house. You picture each turn and road in your mind's eye as you give the directions. And that is how I captured a process I didn't realize I had.

Two Things You Need to Improve

If you feel that the decorating doesn't come naturally to you, there is hope. I used to work with an instructional designer who told me something one day that rocked my world. She said that you can learn anything if you know two things, just two things.

1. The first thing you need to know is when you are doing "it" wrong.

2. The second thing you need to know is how to fix "it."

As a self-taught photographer, because I used these principles, I first looked at my photos. The really bad ones got me excited because I knew I would learn the most from them. I would pore over each one. What was wrong with it? That list of what was wrong was long—overexposed, underexposed, blurry, disjointed, boring, yada, yada, yada. Then I would ask myself what I should have done differently. Those were the things I tried the next time. Most of the time my corrections fixed the problem. But when they didn't, I kept trying new things until I was satisfied that the photo was "done." It was a slow process, but by making every mistake possible, you learn a lot that a teacher can't teach you.

While it is true that some people are more talented than others, I believe that with a bit of study and practice, we can all improve. This is why I recommend that you photograph your rooms. The photographs will tell you what is working and what isn't. The first step is being able to identify what isn't working in your room. Sometimes you *know* what isn't working, but you don't want to know. The kind of things you don't want to know about include that large chair you just bought that is too big for your room, the pillow that is the wrong shade of blue, and the artwork that gives you the creeps every time you walk past it. These are just some of the decorating mistakes I have made along my decorating journey. It is because of the thousands of mistakes I have made that I am qualified to talk about décor. I think I have made just about every mistake you can make, and I have learned from them.

Guidelines

Decorating is about creating a home you love that loves you back. I am not going to tell you that you can't do this and you can't do that. I don't like rules. But guidelines are like highway signs, pointing you in the direction you want to go.

1. Avoid the fads.

Remember when ducks were popular in decorating (probably before your time)? Everyone had ducks in their décor, or maybe it was just my mom. Then just as quickly as they came into fashion, they went out, and my mom was stuck with a house full of dated ducks. I'm not sure she even liked the creatures. So even if "everyone is doing it," don't, unless the look really appeals to you. Because when it goes "out" (and it will), you will be stuck with it. If it was a fad that is over, selling it (both the home and the dated furnishings in it) will be difficult. And really, do you want your house to look exactly like everyone else's house? Another example is all of the projects I see made with pallets. I am not crazy about the look, so I never jumped on this bandwagon. I don't care if I miss a trend. If I don't like it, I'm not doing it. Now on the other hand, when I saw the trend of using grain sacks I jumped on that train, because I love them. They are historic. Many of mine date to the 1800's or earlier. They hold up well and have a look that is impossible to replicate with new fabric. If the look goes out, I am prepared to keep mine. That is what I mean about being selective about what fad or trend you follow.

2. Don't be afraid to be different.

If you see a look you like, then I think it is great to try to recreate your version of the look in your own home. I just want to encourage you to put your own spin on the look. Incorporate your collection of vintage ribbon or that old pitcher grandma gave you. Try to give the look a twist with your personality.

You have a unique style, and I want to encourage you to develop it. Find things you like, whether they are "popular" trends or not. If everyone is going blue and you like red, then go red! My grandmother loved red, and she had a red bedroom even in a day and time when only brothels were red! Well, she didn't care, and I applaud her for taking her own path. If you love Moroccan style, for example, then I say do what makes your heart sing, and don't worry about what everyone else is doing. The exception to this rule (excuse me, guideline) is when we are talking about the house itself and not the décor. Houses are so expensive, and most of us are very concerned about resale. So hold off on wild selections when selecting flooring, tile, countertops, and really any big-ticket items that will stay with the house, so they will appeal to many buyers. But as for your sofa, lamps, towels, and tables—buy what you love.

3. Think outside the box.

I wanted a Mora clock, also known as a Swedish grandfather clock—and I mean I *really* wanted one. I saw them at Round Top for about $2,000 each. The price was for an antique clock that had been refurbished, meaning the clock worked. I actually think that is a good price compared to some I have seen online, but I still couldn't justify paying that much for a clock. Instead, I looked for a reproduction clock and found one. There was just one problem. It was black. It looked sturdy, and had a nice shape, but I really didn't like the color. The black color made it look contemporary, and I wanted it to look antique. So I bought it, tried out the black for about three days (that was as long as I could stand it) and then painted it gray. I love it now! So if you find something that you like, but it isn't quite right, think about if you could paint or change it to suit your own taste and style.

4. Don't go matchy-matchy.

I used to really like matchy-matchy everything. If I liked the chair, then I wanted the sofa, the end table, the coffee table, the chair and settee to match it. I remember hearing that matchy-matchy was bad because then your house would look like a catalog photo for a furniture store. I thought, *What's wrong with that? I would LOVE for my home to look as good as a catalog.* Then as I got older, I finally agreed with that sentiment. Catalog rooms look nice, but they don't look like someone lives there. They don't have a soul. I want a real home, one that looks like it evolved over time. I don't want a room that looks like I bought it all in one day at the same place. If things match too much, they can be boring and feel flat.

5. Add the unexpected.

Maybe it's just the artist in me, but I like to have something unexpected in my home that is unique. Usually I like to add at least one thing to each room. So for my living room, I used an old iron fence post as the newel post on our stairway. I used empty frames on the wall in my dining room, and put sconces in the center of each one. In the bedroom, I hung my wedding dress and my mother-in-law's old dress on the end of my armoire. I made our large walk-in closet a study. I remember reading about a designer who used to hold dinner parties in his bathroom. I admit it sounded a bit gross to me at the time (I might be a bit of a germaphobe) but when I saw the bathroom (it was amazing), I thought, *Okay, I might be able to eat in here! Now that is totally unexpected!!*

6. Create your own style.

I love the style of many decorators, but I don't try to copy them. I love Charles Faudree's style. I adore it! He used layer upon layer, and each room is overflowing with French antiques. If I tried to copy his style, it would flop. I just don't have that much "good stuff." At best I will only be a good imitator of Charles Faudree, but with my own style I shine; I am the expert. Be your own expert. Embrace your own style. Think about the mood you want to create. How would you describe your style? I used to think about if I wanted a grand, impressive style or a cozy, cottage style. I decided that I wanted a home that embraced rather than impressed.

Some of my style has just evolved organically over time, but some of it, the warmth, the coziness, has been something I consciously chose to create. Think through about the kind of home you want to create. Then choose pieces that support or at least don't fight with your long-term vision for your home.

7. Create a focal point.

A focal point is where your eye travels in a room. Each room has a focal point. Sometimes it is what you want people to see, and other times it is not. This is where their eye goes as they enter the room. Normally this is the wall that one first sees as one enters the room. So what I am saying is to put your best "stuff" here. I want to wow people as soon as they walk into a room. If I had a "blow your mind" painting, I would want it to be the first thing you notice as you enter the room. Putting the best thing on the far wall as you enter the room isn't always possible because of the room layout. If that back wall is a wall of windows, then that is probably not the best place to hang your favorite painting or place your favorite armoire. However, you

should still have the best view as you enter a room. Think of arranging the room so that the first impression one has of the room is the best it can be.

8. Don't line up furniture like soldiers.

We've all seen the expansive living room where the owners weren't sure what to do with the space, so they pushed everything against the walls. It ends up looking a bit like a cold, impersonal space. The chairs and sofa are so far apart from each other, that you feel you must shout to have a conversation. Be sure to put chairs close enough together that you feel you could have a pleasant conversation. If the room is large, you may be able to set up more than one conversation area in the room. It really is okay to move furniture so that it isn't all up against a wall. Our living room and kitchen are one big space, so it really would not have worked to push everything to the exterior walls. The kitchen is behind the sofa. I moved the sofa and settees

Antique garden post converted into a stair newel post

close enough together for intimate conversation, and so I could put my feet on the ottoman no matter where I sit.

9. Let the light shine in.

Although heavy drapes certainly may be French, in today's modern home, most people really like light-flooded rooms. I know we sometimes need to close drapes, shutters, or blinds to protect fabrics when we aren't using the room, for privacy, or to keep the cold out. Still, when I am home, I like to have as much light streaming in as possible. That sunlight has a positive effect on my outlook, and makes the whole room look cheery. If you do have old heavy drapes on a window, I would consider removing them. Nothing dates a room like curtains that are past their prime.

Outdoor bistro chairs make for a cozy seating area to enjoy an afternoon cup of tea by the window.

10. Hang artwork at the correct height.

You want to be able to see artwork without craning your neck. Make sure it is at eye-level if you want your guests to truly appreciate it. Most homeowners hang their art too high on the wall. If paintings or photography are hung over a chest or piece of furniture, then you want the artwork to feel connected to the furniture, so hang it eight inches or less above the furniture. A big gap between artwork and the console or chest below, makes the artwork appear disjointed from the furniture below it. In the photo on page 34, you can see the artwork was hung right above the bed. The top of the artwork also aligns with the top of the drapery hardware.

11. De-clutter.

Nothing ruins a room faster than clutter and too much stuff. We collectors are especially guilty of this one. If the room feels crowded, you won't like it, and neither will guests. If your room feels or looks crowded, the solution is easy and usually free. Remove something! Look around the room. What don't you like? What doesn't work in the room? Take those things out. If it is furniture, and it doesn't work in another room, then give it away or consign it. I know from my days developing statistic courses that you need lots of white space on a page. Too much information on a page feels overwhelming. A room operates the same way. You want the eye to rest in between the beautiful things in your room.

12. Select paint color last.

I suggest you pick out your paint last, because there are thousands of shades, and really the options are endless. Fabric choices (at least in patterns and colors I like) are very limited. It will be much easier to find paint that works with your fabrics than it will be to find fabrics that go with your paint. Also, I suggest going with a more neutral paint color, so if you change your color scheme, you won't be forced to paint each time. I've learned that one the hard way. The other reason to choose your paint last is that you really need to see the fabrics and colors in the room to see what will work together. Lighting is tricky and different in every room. People don't often realize just how different light sources can cause colors to look different. Being a photographer, I am very aware of the blue cast from daylight and a camera flash. Incandescent bulbs and a setting sun give off a

golden light, while fluorescent lighting has a green cast. If the fabrics are in the room, then it is easier to check the paint color in the room's actual lighting, rather than store lighting. Be sure to look at the paint samples during the day and in the evening. A sample is easily applied to the wall so you can check the shade. Or better yet, try three or five or seven shades all at the same time. If you don't want to test paint samples on the wall, try painting on a large board.

13. Use a limited color palette.

I try to use no more than two or at most three prominent colors in a room. If there are too many different colors, the room can feel confusing. Not only are too many colors sometimes too much for a room, it's also important to balance the color in a room. One room of mine started out green. I changed the bedding to blue, but still had some green accents on the other side of the room. In taking some photos of a room recently, I realized that one side of the room was blue and cream, while the other side of the room was mainly green and yellow. It wasn't until I saw the photos that I realized the two photos looked like they were taken in two different rooms. Had I not photographed the room, I wouldn't have realized how much the painting didn't work in the room. Of course, when you work with neutrals, you don't have to worry about having too many patterns and colors. If you keep the colors to a minimum, that will automatically give the

room a cohesive look, even if you did nothing else. Using just a few colors can unify a room, while using many can make a room feel busy and stressful. The fewer colors in the room, the easier it is to decorate.

14. Limit the number of patterns in a room.

Using more than one pattern is fine. Just keep in mind that patterns make the decorating process more complicated. You'll want to vary the pattern size, so that maybe you have one large print, and you can pair it with a smaller, simpler pattern. It's always easy to add a check or stripe to the pattern mix. Be sure your colors all work together and keep the number of prominent colors to a minimum

15. Add color with accent pieces.

Nothing says cozy and "come sit here" like a chair or sofa with pillows. Just be sure not to overdo it. This is also a great way to add an accent color or pattern to the room in small doses. Throws are a great way to add color or pattern to a room, and they can easily be cleaned or replaced when needed.

16. Use attractive, decorative items for storage.

If you must keep certain items, like TV remotes, in plain view, then organize them into a basket or box, so that they at least look neat. If I have a choice of storing something in a plastic bin or an attractive wire basket, I am going to choose the wire basket every time.

17. Only buy things you love.

Only buy things you love. If you buy things just because they are "the thing" or because they are the right color, you will soon tire of them. When you change color schemes, or when the thing you bought goes out of style, you will no longer like it. But if you bought it because you loved it, you will want to keep it anyway. It's okay to have an eclectic style (a little bit of this and a little bit of that). Often these rooms work because they are full of interesting things. Having one or just a few colors can help unify a room of seemingly disparate objects.

18. Add lights and darks.

My mother is painter. She taught me about oil paintings, and I remember she said that you need lights and darks in each painting. It's interesting how an idea that works well in one visual medium works in others as well. When photographing, I try to have lights and darks in my photos, and I think a room needs both. We've all seen a room where everything is white. I love white, but I don't want every surface in a room to be white. If you have a white table, then try using chairs that are not painted. If your walls are white, then go with a dark stain on your wood floors. Those are just a few of the ways to add lights and darks. Although I have painted a lot of furniture in my day, I don't want all of my furniture to be painted. I like seeing the stained wood. If you are using white furniture in the room, make sure you have at least one piece that isn't painted white.

This dark console is paired beautifully with the light horse artwork.

19. Use similar color palettes in nearby rooms.

It is jarring to go from a room of pastels to a room of vivid colors. You want all of your rooms to feel that they complement each other. If you look at pictures from different rooms in your house, do they look like they are all in the same house? Or do they look like they belong in different houses? You want things to flow from one room to another. I suggest for a "decorator" look, that your rooms have a similar feel. The colors don't have to be the same, but the rooms need to feel like they were all designed by the same person. For example, if you love a French look, try to have something French in all of your rooms. If you love bold colors, then I think the whole house will work best with bold colors throughout.

20. Don't fear mistakes.

Don't worry that you will make a mistake. I can tell you right now, you will! It will happen. But the good news is that you will also learn from your mistakes. I learn more from my mistakes than I do from my successes. When I have a success, sometimes I don't know why it worked, so I am not sure how to replicate it. But when I make a mistake, I can usually tell you what I did wrong. And that means I probably won't make that mistake again. I am constantly experimenting. Some of my ideas end up looking awful, and I don't worry about those, so long as they are reversible. I don't take chances with big ticket items or big purchases that

Oyster baskets are a great way to corral things like towels.

cannot be returned. But there's no harm in buying a few pillows that end up not working. I simply return them or move them to another room. Sometimes I buy something I adore and it just doesn't work in the room I bought it for. In this case, I don't worry, because I really, really liked the item. I simply try it in different room until I find a place it works. If you try something and it doesn't work, try to figure out why. Experiment, and you will greatly improve your decorating muscles.

21. Shop your house.

Rather than running to the store when you need something, check your closets, the attic, and other rooms in your home. This is a major blogger trick. If you want to give a room new life, first try moving things around from one room to another. I often get a fresh look by simply rotating things around the house. It is free and doesn't require you to leave the house. You can do this step in your PJs. Sometimes a thing that didn't work in one spot will be perfect in another. If you don't move things around, you'll never know. If I can't find a home for something, it goes out the door to someone else. I shop my house all of the time.

22. Use the rule of three.

Three is a good number for decorating. There's just something magical about it. When you see an arrangement that is visually pleasing, often the secret ingredient is the

number three. If you have one candlestick, it usually works better if you have three. Or maybe you have three things in a vignette and each item is different. Think of the front of a house with a planter on either side of the front door. That's a set of three things. When adding accessories, three is a great number, so try adding three candlesticks, three plates on the wall, three pitchers, three books, or three potted plants. Maybe it's two lamps and a clock in the middle. Odd numbers often work best in décor, and three seems to be the odd number that most often works.

Right: These photos showcase an example of experimentation. I've changed out the art above my bed so many times to find just the right look. I finally settled on the French mirror and ironstone platters. Although some readers don't care for the look, it speaks to me.

CHAPTER 4:
THE FARMHOUSE FRENCH LIST

There really isn't a formula to follow for creating a Farmhouse French room. I see so many beautiful French rooms, all unique and as individual as a snowflake. They are all so different, so "one of a kind" and lovely. What works for one owner in one room won't necessarily work for another owner or another room. I think suggesting that you should make your home fit some sort of mold would be doing you a disservice. I really do aim for you to showcase your interests, your personality, and talents in your home so that it shows off your charm. I don't want it to look like a cookie-cutter house. I want your guests to walk into your home and feel at once that it is as unique and beautiful as you are. I want them to feel the warmth and love in your home, but to also sense a quiet elegance. I don't like a one-size-fits-all approach. Having said that, there are some tricks of the trade that will go a long way to help you achieve a French look in your home without spending a fortune. These are the items I often suggest to my clients, both personal and professional. The items don't need to be "made in France" to work. That is the beauty of this list. I have baskets from craft stores that look amazingly expensive and French.

Here is my go-to list for things to create a Farmhouse French look:

1. French chair—or better yet, two!

If you can't find a French chair, go with a curvy one. Often, it just needs a bit of flourish to give that feeling of elegance to a room. Many Italian

Right: This French chair was re-covered using Italian linen.

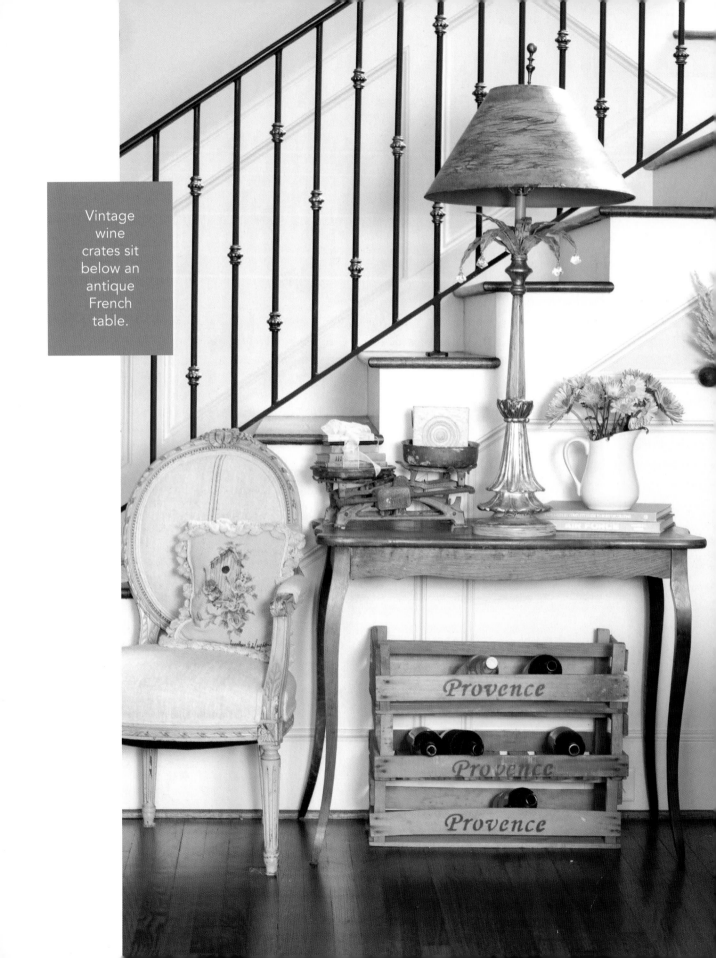

Vintage
wine
crates sit
below an
antique
French
table.

chairs will work quite well. In fact, many of the craftsmen that made furniture for French royalty were Italian. Adding a French or French-ish (curvy) chair is by far the easiest way to add "Frenchiness" (made-up word) to a room. Just one small French curvy chair gives visitors a clue that this room has a French accent.

2. French side table

French tables are a bit more difficult to come by, but certainly they are out there. Curvy furniture adds a French flair to a room. It may be difficult to tell if a box or basket is French, but it is usually quite easy to tell if a chair or table is French.

3. French mirror

I feel like I am repeating myself, but ditto on the mirrors; curvy works, even if the mirror isn't officially French. The good news is that French mirrors are fairly easy to find. Mirrors are great additions to most rooms, so why not add one with lots of curves and personality? They reflect light and can make a room feel more spacious.

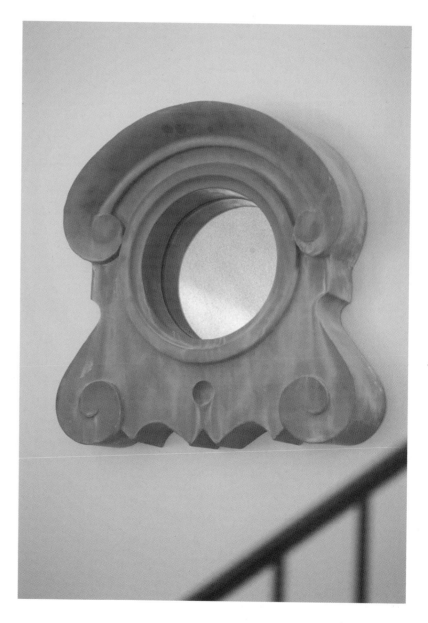

4. Chandelier, wood, or crystal

A chandelier really does such elegance to a room. I hope you will use at least one in your home. We live in the South, where the heat can be oppressive in the summer, so we use a lot of ceiling fans. Where we don't need the fans, I try to use chandeliers as much as possible. We've used them in the kitchen, dining room, bathroom, closet, laundry room, and on the back porch. Be creative! And if you don't have electricity where you want to hang a chandelier, try using a non-electric one that uses candles.

5. Rustic beamed ceiling

I know what you are thinking. If your house doesn't already have a beamed ceiling, you may think it is too late to add beams. Check with your carpenter. It may be cheaper and easier than you think. Any crown molding might need to be removed, but that's not a difficult job for most professionals.

6. Woven baskets, especially rectangular-shaped baskets

Baskets are incredibly easy to find. The difficulty lies in finding pretty ones that look antique or vintage. Look for vintage baskets at antique and resale shops. If you can't find good antique baskets, try looking for new baskets in gray tones. Square or rectangular baskets work great for stacking. Try stenciling numbers on rectangular baskets for a cool vintage look.

7. Dough bowls

Dough bowls or troughs are perfect for holding seasonal items like pumpkins in the fall, moss balls in the spring, bunches of lavender in the summer, or pinecones in the winter.

8. Bread boards

Bread boards are gorgeous and look fantastic displayed in so many ways. I love hanging them on the wall like art. You can stack them on your fireplace mantle or use them flat on your kitchen island covered with vases of flowers or bowls of fruit.

9. Wood totes and crates

Wood totes or crates often evoke a country French feel. Antique or new, it doesn't matter, they give a room warmth and an organic feel. I

often use wood crates to display books or hold extra pillows. But even the small, inexpensive wood totes can add a bit of atmosphere.

10. Wood Trays

Trays are the perfect accessory for almost any room. I love to use them on my ottoman to display a stack of favorite books or a vase of flowers. They work so well on a table to corral items you have on display. Trays are also nice when used to serve food, or carry plates outdoors when having a party. I have a stack of wood trays we use at the farm for carrying food outdoors.

11. French script or ephemera on anything

There are many items available these days with French writing on them, but you can also make your own. You can use stencils or other transfer techniques. My friend Karen, the Graphics Fairy (TheGraphicsFairy.com) has lots of free graphics and shares her techniques for adding the graphic to just about anything.

Toile bedding with shutter doors behind the bed

12. Silver pitchers

Silver pitchers are so beautiful and add so much bling to a room. The good news is that they tarnish. Yes, that is the *good news*. Because they tarnish, people get rid of their silverware by the truckloads. That means there are massive amounts of silver-plate pitchers for sale. A silver-plated pitcher is the perfect vase for flowers cut from your yard, or for a $5 bouquet from the grocery store. Displaying your grocery store flowers in a silver pitcher will elevate them to a whole new level. Go ahead, try it and see for yourself.

13. Silverware

I do love using silverware for meals. It does require extra care, so I don't use it all of the time. I do, however, use a silver spoon for my morning tea every day. Does it taste better? You bet! Now let's say you don't end up using silverware for meals, but I hope you do. It also looks super fabulous stored in an ironstone pitcher, even if you don't actually use it. I don't mind if it tarnishes, but I try to polish my silver every six months or when I think of it. If you use your silver regularly, you won't actually need to polish it.

14. Textured fabric like homespun linen, or drop cloth

Although traditional French fabrics were often cheery bright colors, like blue and yellow, these neutral fabrics were still used for bedding and other purposes. My favorite fabric to work with is linen, but sometimes I use burlap and drop cloth fabric. You can do amazing things with drop cloth. If you sew, you can use these fabrics in amazing ways. You

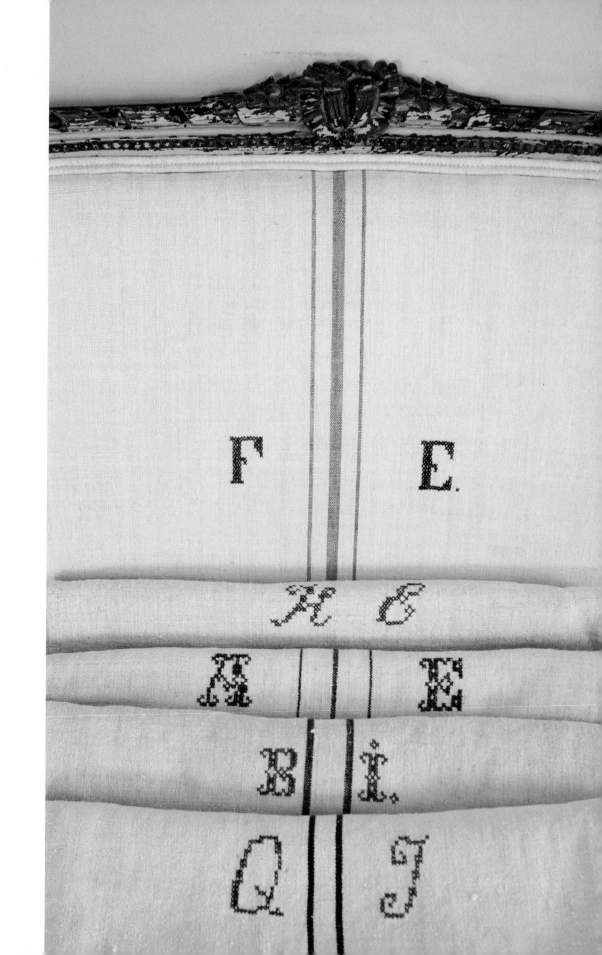

can make curtains, slipcovers, tablecloths, bedding, chair cushions, and pillows just to name a few. When selecting pre-made curtains or bed linens, you can always choose linen. Linen does tend to be more expensive, but it is well worth it. I would rather have one set of good sheets than fifty so-so sets.

15. Grain sacks

Grain sacks are one of my very favorite things. The easiest way to use them is to stuff one with a king-size pillow. The king-size pillows are typically the right size for most grain sacks. If you find your grain sack is too big for a king-size pillow, try a body pillow. Then you have a nice long pillow that can be used on a bed, or a sofa or settee. Grain sacks are perfect for so many reasons. The fabric is nubby and gorgeous, they usually have a very pretty stripe or several stripes. Some even sport a monogram. The fabric is sturdy and usually holds up to hard wear. I use them for upholstery, making pillows, table runners, and even placemats.

16. Traditional French fabrics like tapestry, toile, and stripes

What is French ticking? Ticking refers to a striped fabric typically used to make mattresses. A blue-striped fabric is often referred to as French ticking, because they used a blue-striped fabric on their mattresses. Now, I often hear that term used to refer to any simple blue-and-white striped fabric. It is beautiful in its simplicity. There are several new fabrics to choose from and products made with this type of fabric. Toile is a very traditional French fabric that usually shows bucolic scenes. There are many beautiful French fabrics.

17. White ironstone platters

Of course I prefer real ironstone, made in England, but there are some beautiful new pieces available also. I don't think any of my ironstone is actually made in France, but it still gives a room an old feel, which reminds me of France and the French countryside.

18. French dishes like Quimper

Quimper plates say "French" like few things do. They are quintessential country French, but also difficult to find. They are usually colorful, so if you want to introduce color into a room, this might be a great way to go.

19. Chippy paint

If you love antiques, then it follows that you might like things with chippy paint. I love old things, things with history, especially if they have a worn finish. I love to imagine who owned them, how they were used, all of the details of their lives. You can even antique new pieces to give them an antique feel. Old furniture with chippy paint is a great way to add detail to a room. Now let me clarify that when I was in Paris, I saw no furniture that was worn and chippy. There were furniture pieces in the high-end shops with lots of gilding, but no chipped paint. The chippy paint gives a room the feeling of faded elegance, of inherited pieces, and that

The rustic finish of these iron lamps works well with the reclaimed tin.

certainly can add a country French feel to a room. As I said earlier, I don't want to put French design in a box. You can definitely have a French room without anything chippy in there.

20. Gold mirrors

Gold frames and gold mirrors are two examples of a way to bring in gilded wood. You can even paint something yourself if you like.

21. Gesso frames

Gesso frames are almost always vintage or antique. I don't think they make them any more. Often the gesso has broken off in places and there are chips. These

imperfections add to the patina. I love using them in a room. I don't paint them, but let the original chipped finish show. The frames can be empty, since they are a work of art on their own.

22. Angels

I just love angels. I think they have an old-world feel, and they work beautifully with Farmhouse French style. Why not use them in your home?

23. Santos

I have reproduction Santos, but originally they were made for Catholic churches in very remote areas in Spain. They were used to convert indigenous people. They are also called cage dolls. The cage was added to better hold and shape the vestments that the

santos typically wore. Real antique santos can be very expensive, but the reproduction ones like I have are much more reasonable although difficult to find.

24. Old clocks

Old clocks have a look that is very hard to find in new clocks. So many of the old clocks have amazing detail that is so beautiful. Some of the French clocks have charming figures and I have an art Noveau clock that has many swirls and embellishments. They are not currently working, but that's what your smart phone is for. Use the clocks to add fabulous details to your room.

25. Vintage scales

Each set of scales I find is so different. The most unique one I found is a French postal scale. It has gold details and is very delicate. Other scales are large. Some come with the weights intact, but many no longer have the weights. They are perfect for displaying fruit or other goodies in your kitchen.

26. Tureens

I am crazy about dishes, and tureens are some of my favorite dishes. There are so many shapes that they come in. Some are long and short, while others are tall and narrow. I especially love the hand-painted ones. My favorite is a lavender and white one given to us as a wedding present. (It was my favorite wedding gift.)

27. Finials

Most of the finials I own are reproductions. They certainly don't need to be the real deal to be amazing. The real ones are often quite large, so be sure you take the dimensions into consideration before buying one online.

28. Candelabras

You can find vintage candelabras with crystals. Newer ones tend to be more plain. Either way, they have an old-world charm I love.

29. China Teapots

Did I say that tureens were my favorite type of dish? I meant teapots. It's so hard to decide which is my favorite. I had so many teapots at one time that my house was overrunning with them. I sold most of them and only kept my favorites. I love to display them, but I also use them every day. I have tea every morning.

30. Silver Teapots

Sometimes these are sold as a set with the coffee pot, a sugar, creamer, and a tray. I also find the teapots sold as orphans. I like displaying the teapots, especially the older styles. They work well throughout the house.

31. Silver trays

Silver trays add such elegance to a room. They are great for displaying elements in an elegant way. I use mine to carry my Saturday breakfast out to the porch. I think everyone needs a silver tray so they can feel pampered.

32. Seltzer bottles

They come in clear, green, blue glass, and sometimes other colors. They look nice in the kitchen, and other places. I like to display mine in open shelving in my kitchen.

33. Crystal bowls

I display crystal bowls on open shelving, but the bowls are also great to display fruit or other goodies. Display them where the sun hits them for full sparkly effect.

34. Crystal pitchers

Crystal pitchers are great for displaying flowers or you can leave them empty. Large or small, they look fabulous.

35. Cake stands

Cake stands are always fabulous. I love the crystal ones, glass ones, and porcelain ones. They look great when you are serving food, but I also love showing them off in my glass-fronted kitchen cabinets.

36. Boxwood wreaths

Some people just display boxwood wreaths at Christmas time, but I love to use them year-round. They add color and something organic to your room. I prefer the real preserved boxwood wreaths to the fake ones. They are expensive, but they last a long time.

37. Moss balls

These are easy to make. I start with Styrofoam balls, then use hot glue to add the moss to the balls. They look fantastic in dough bowls and on top of candlesticks. If you prefer, they can also be purchased.

38. Lambs

I love lambs and love to use them in my home. Some of them are from church nativity crèche sets.

39. Enamel pitchers

Enamel pitchers from France are especially lovely. They come in many colors, but I prefer the white and blue ones.

40. Candlesticks

I have an assortment of very old candlesticks and new ones. I like to display an assortment of candlesticks of varying heights and designs. I especially love the wood ones and the silver ones.

41. Fish set

A fish set is a set of forks and knives made for use in a fish course. Most people don't have a fish course anymore. I buy them because of their unique look. They are super fun to display. The handles are typically cellulose or bone. I love the handles, since they have such a unique look.

42. Champagne buckets

Champagne buckets are perfect for so many things. They are great for chilling champagne of course, but they also look great holding a moss or boxwood ball. You can use them as a vase also. I've used them to hold guest towels in the powder room too.

43. Trophies

Trophies have the look of something handed down over time. They tend to look like heirlooms, even if you bought yours at a consignment store. I use one for holding my makeup brushes and another one to hold my reading glasses. They can also be used as a flower vase or to display a moss or boxwood ball.

44. Busts

Almost all busts I see are vintage. I don't think there are too many made these days. They definitely have a nod to the past, and I am fascinated by them. I always wonder about who they represent. Typically, they are quite reasonably priced.

45. Vintage portraits

The portraits also fascinate me. I like to think about the people pictured. Were they happy? Where did they live? What did they do? What were their interests? I prefer the original paintings, but prints are great too.

46. Florentine accents pieces

I often find Florentine trays pretty easily. I also love using Florentine tissue boxes, jewelry chests, and trinket boxes. Every

now and then, I can find a Florentine table or a set of stacking tables. They have become quite popular ,so the price has gone up significantly over the years.

Vintage stacking Florentine tables can really add a bit of Italian flourish to the room.

47. Ironwork

Rusty or non-rusty, beautiful ironwork is also something that has a French feel. Perhaps it is the porch railings I remember seeing in New Orleans, ironwork makes me think of French design. You can incorporate iron into a room by adding something . . . well . . . iron, like iron lamps, or an iron door stop, or even iron stair railing. Sometimes you can find a bit of iron fencing to add somewhere.

48. Ruffled pillows

Ruffles are a way to add softness and feminine charm without using floral patterns. I love using a few ruffled pillows, especially in a bedroom. Men seem to find the ruffles more tolerable than floral fabrics too.

49. Linen bedding

Linen bedding is such a luxury, but it is well worth it in my opinion. Linen is a natural fabric that holds up over time. I love using soft, muted colors with a long drop bedspread.

50. Painted furniture

Much of French furniture from the Louis XVI period was originally painted, so yes I associate painted furniture with French design. I like having a few painted pieces in each room, but I prefer to have a mix, rather than using all painted furniture in a room. If everything is white for example, it all begins to blend together. You need some contrast in a room.

51. Bottles

Old bottles are perfect for so many reasons. The wavy glass is beautiful and gives an old presence to a room. It looks collected over time. The other thing I love about old bottles is that they are usually clear and they go with any color décor.

52. Cloches

Cloches feel old-world to me. I also love how they can make a room feel like a conservatory. Add some plants and it feels like a Victorian green house. Like the bottles, they go with any color décor. You can add seasonal elements underneath the cloche and change them out each season. I love to add an ivy or moisture-loving plant under mine. They usually thrive and don't require you to water them as often.

53. Slipcovers

I like to think of the families in the nineteenth-century heading to their summer homes. They would cover their furniture with white sheets to protect it from the sun and dust. Slipcovers often remind me of those white sheets draped on the furniture. But also slipcovers are practical and can be easily removed and washed. White ones can usually be bleached.

54. Vintage books

Vintage books remind me of old family libraries full of books that have been collected over time, and maybe generations. We've got a large collection of books from my father-in-law's collection. He was the dean of a seminary and has a wonderful collection of theology books including many texts in Hebrew, Greek, and French.

55. Dried lavender

It's so "French" and smells heavenly. I use the bundles all over my home. I even keep a bowl of lavender in my bathroom. I stir it anytime I want that wonderful lavender scent.

56. Monogrammed linen towels

I am not sure what it is about a monogram, but I am crazy for them. The reality is I don't care if it's my monogram or not. I just love the artistry of monogrammed linens.

57. Monogrammed hand towels

I prefer the vintage linen sheets and hand towels, but I love all monogrammed hand towels

58. Linen napkins

I love to use linen napkins when we have guests. There's something about having a real napkins for guests that feels so luxurious these days. Go ahead, try it next time you have guests. Yes they will need to be laundered, but as a special treat, it's so worth it.

59. Floral frogs

Floral frogs are those metal pieces that go in the bottom of a vase to hold the flower stems in place. They are charming stacked or even placed in a bowl. The best part is that you can use them as intended in a vase any time you like.

60. Cake, butter, and chocolate molds

The molds were originally used to mold foods like chocolate or cake or butter, but they are also gorgeous displayed on a shelf. I bought one in the shape of a lamb. They are so charming to use in your home décor and not just in your kitchen.

61. Rolling pins

A collection of old and new rolling pins is perfect for a kitchen. I display mine in an old butter churn.

62. Silver hand mirrors

Silver hand mirrors look luxurious sitting on a vanity, but would also be fantastic displayed as a grouping on the wall.

I have used everything on this list at one time or another. French style is subtle and requires a subtle approach. You don't need a room full of fleur-de-lis, or roosters, or the Eiffel tower to "announce" that a room is French. Let the room speak for itself softly and elegantly.

CHAPTER 5: WHERE TO SHOP

It is one thing to know what you need to buy. It is quite another task to find a place that sells it. It is difficult to find vintage items for your home in certain parts of the country, and it is also difficult to find reasonably priced French things. However, it can be done. There are many places you can shop online and locally. I cannot guarantee you will have great shops near your home, but there are lots of online options available to you.

ONLINE SOURCES	
I have bought from or worked with all of these online stores.	
Aidan Gray	• Lamps throughout house
American Tin Ceilings	• Tin behind bed at farm
Amy Howard at Home	• Gilding on vanity in bathroom
Antropologie	• Doggy robe hooks in city master bath
Bali Blinds	• Blinds throughout city house • Blinds throughout guest quarters • City master drapes
Ballard Designs	• Rug in city study • Rug in city living room • Curtains in city dining room • Wall décor behind city master bed • Candle sconce on wall of city master bedroom

Bella Notte	• Linen bedspread, pillow shams, and velvet bolster at the farm
Birch Lane	• Rug in farm living room • Chairs in farm living room
Blinds.com	• Blinds in the guest quarters
Build.com	• City kitchen island chandeliers • City closet chandelier
Calico	• Fabrics for guest room throw • Bolster and pillows • Slipcovers in dining room
Carpet One	• Rugs in farm bedrooms
Dash and Albert	• Rug in city dining room • Rug in breakfast room
Décor Steals	• Many of the white plates and platters in the city breakfast room plate rack • Bamboo rug in guest quarters • Some of the white cake plates in city kitchen • Glass front cabinets
Garnet Hill	• Master bedroom linen sheets
Heritage Lace	• Much of the lace shown, including the lace panels in the city powder room
Horchow	• City dining room chandelier

Home Goods	• Many of the white dishes in the glass front dishes in the kitchen cabinets • Chairs at the farm kitchen table • Tufted chair in city girl's room
Joss and Main	• Swedish clock, bench in city dining room
Layla Grayce	• Pillows on city master bed
Lighting Direct	• City kitchen island chandeliers • City closet chandelier
Overstock	• Wool blue ottoman in city girl's bedroom
Pottery Barn	• Bed skirt on guest quarters bed • Curtain rods in city master bedroom
Restoration Hardware	• City kitchen island French counter stools • City dining room table • City dining room console • Farm living room daybed

Rustica Hardware	• Hanging hardware for city barn doors to study
Soft Surroundings	• Brass folding tables in city house • Chests in Evangeline's room • Side tables in the city living room
Southern Honey Chalk Paint	• Used extensively, many of the pieces were painted with this paint including the Swedish clock, the French cupboard in the guest quarters, and the iron bed in the guest quarters
Superior Custom Linens	• Linen blanket in the city master bedrooms • Sheets at the farm
Target	• Large green bottle in guest quarters
Thermador	• 48-inch gas range in city house kitchen
Turkish T	• Towels, hand towel, and lavender robes by the city master pedestal tub • Blue striped towel in city powder room • White tablecloth used on city dining room table
Vintage Tub and Bath	• Pedestal tub in the city master bath • Clawfoot tub in the city powder room
Wisteria	• Column table by bed in guest quarters • Sofa table in city living room • Farm kitchen table
World Market	• Chair at vanity in city master bedroom • Furniture at treehouse

Local Sources

Although I enjoy the convenience of shopping online, I also love going into local stores, where you can touch and see the merchandise in person. In high-end boutiques, antique shops, and thrift shops, you can sit in a chair, touch the fabric, and see for yourself the difference between a Louis XV and a Louis XVI chair. Here you learn. You can ask the shopkeeper why one piece is more expensive than another. The owners are usually quite knowledgeable, and you can learn so much from them. I shop a lot at resale shops, but also love to go into high-end boutiques. There I get ideas and sometimes make a purchase. With sales, there are sometimes deals to be had. You won't know unless you check them out in person though. Be sure to ask whether they ever give discounts or when sales might be occurring. Don't be embarrassed to ask. Trust me, you won't be the only one asking.

HERE'S A LIST OF STORES THAT I LOVE TO VISIT IN PERSON:

- *A&G Antique Mall* (facebook.com/AGAntiquesonnWest19th)
- *August Antiques* (bensantiquegardening.com/augusta)
- *Heights Antiques on Yale* (heightsantiques.com)
- *Jubilee* (jubileeshop.com)
- *Lauries in Tomball* (laurieshomefurnishings.com)
- *Leftovers* (leftoversantiques.net)
- *Stillgoode* (stillgoode.com)
- *Three Doors* (threedoorshouston.com)

Yard Sales

Yard sales are a great place to get a good deal. The down side is they require lots of driving around, and they are a mixed bag. Some will have a lot of what you are looking for, but most won't. If you are on a strict budget and have the time to go, I think they can be fun, and on occasion, you will discover a "pot of gold" find. For me personally, I found that often it was disappointing to have spent my entire morning driving around only to find the kind of stuff that I too was trying to get rid of. I don't have the time or patience anymore to shop yard sales, but who knows, I may be missing all kinds of goodies. If you do go, be sure to go early in the day the first day of the sale. Most yard sales are pretty well picked over if you arrive on day two, or even late in the day on day one.

Auctions

I personally adore attending auctions. Not only do they usually have some good stuff for a decent price, but the bidding is so much fun. Who thought up this method of selling stuff anyway? He must be the most talented salesman ever. To refer to "buying" something as "winning" it is brilliant. When the gavel goes down, and my buyer number is called out, I admit it's quite exhilarating, especially if there has been a bidding war. Of course when you "win it," that means you agreed to buy it for more than anyone else in the room was willing to pay for it. But the bid amount is not what you actually pay for your item. You have to tack on the buyer's premium (a percentage that each auction house adds to your bill) and the tax. If the item is too large for your vehicle, there will be a delivery fee as well.

There are two types of errors you can make at the auction.

1. You can get caught up in the excitement and end up paying much more than you intended.

2. You can be so conservative that you miss out on a one-of-a-kind piece because the price went slightly over a limit you had preset.

So you could end up paying too much for something, or miss out on the opportunity to buy something rare and unique. You have only seconds to decide before the gavel goes down. The error I typically make is letting something get away. I have often regretted not bidding a bit more. As I have said before, as long as you can afford it, buy what you like and walk away from a bargain that is just so-so.

If you would like to attend an auction, here are my auction tips.

1. Find an auction house near you.

Try websites like Auctionzip.com to find auction houses in your zip code or nearby. I wouldn't bother asking antique stores. Often antique stores buy their merchandise there, so they are not going to divulge their source. Antique sources are often guarded closely. We used to purchase antiques from a nearby antique store that carried beautiful antiques. One day, my husband asked the owner where she got her antiques and she gazed into the distance with a wistful look and described fanciful, romantic trips to France to select and purchase her furniture. We were mesmerized. It sounded so exotic and exciting. Years later, I ran into the shop owner at a local auction. Then every time I went, she was there. She narrowed her eyes when she looked at me, so I knew that she knew that I knew. Her secret was out!

2. Preview online.

A lot of auction houses have websites, and typically you can preview the auction online. This is a marvelous service and can save you a lot of time. I still recommend that you inspect the item thoroughly before bidding. The purpose of the online preview is not to inspect the item before bidding, but to determine if the auction is worth your time to attend. If you don't see anything you like, stay home and enjoy doing something else. If you find something you can't live without, you can still check it out thoroughly before the auction. Show up a bit early to check out pieces before the auction begins. You can continue to preview items during the bidding, but it's a bit more difficult. You just risk the auctioneer taking

These rustic pencils by the bed mean you can write down that fabulous dream from last night.

This gorgeous lamp looks right at home in front of a French mirror.

bids on an item you didn't look over yet. You can often bid online and over the phone. If you decide to bid remotely, be sure to call the auction house and ask for a condition report on the piece since you won't be able to inspect it in person.

3. Know the going price.

Bidding is fun, and it is easy to get caught up in the thrill of the moment and with adrenaline rushing, agree to pay a ridiculous price for an old pair of shoes. Auction prices are usually close to wholesale, but that isn't always true. The more people in attendance, the higher the prices are going to be. And if the auction house offers online and phone bidding, you could be bidding against any number of people not in attendance. Make sure to do your homework ahead of time. Know what the item is worth before you bid, and more importantly, know what the item is worth to you. If I know that type of chair or dresser is often available at the antique mall or auction, then I would not be willing to pay over what I know the going price is for that item. If, however, the item is extremely rare and I really, really want it, I would be willing to pay much more. Sometimes the item is so unusual that you can't find it in the store.

Just keep in mind that sometimes bidding gets out of hand, and the price can quickly skyrocket. Know what you can buy the item for in a store. Knowledge is power. If bidding gets out of hand, be prepared to walk away.

4. Know the buyers' premium.

Most auction houses have a buyers' premium. This is a commission, for lack of a better word, that you pay the auction house on top of the bid amount. The auction that I attend most has a buyer's premium of 15%, while another one has a buyers' premium of 20%. They seem to keep going up. Be sure to add in the buyer's premium to the amount you are bidding. So if a chest would sell for $500 at a store, but you can get it for $400 at the auction, is that worth the hassle of attending the auction and having to go on their schedule rather than shopping at your leisure? Let's say you had a winning bid of $400, and then the buyer's premium is

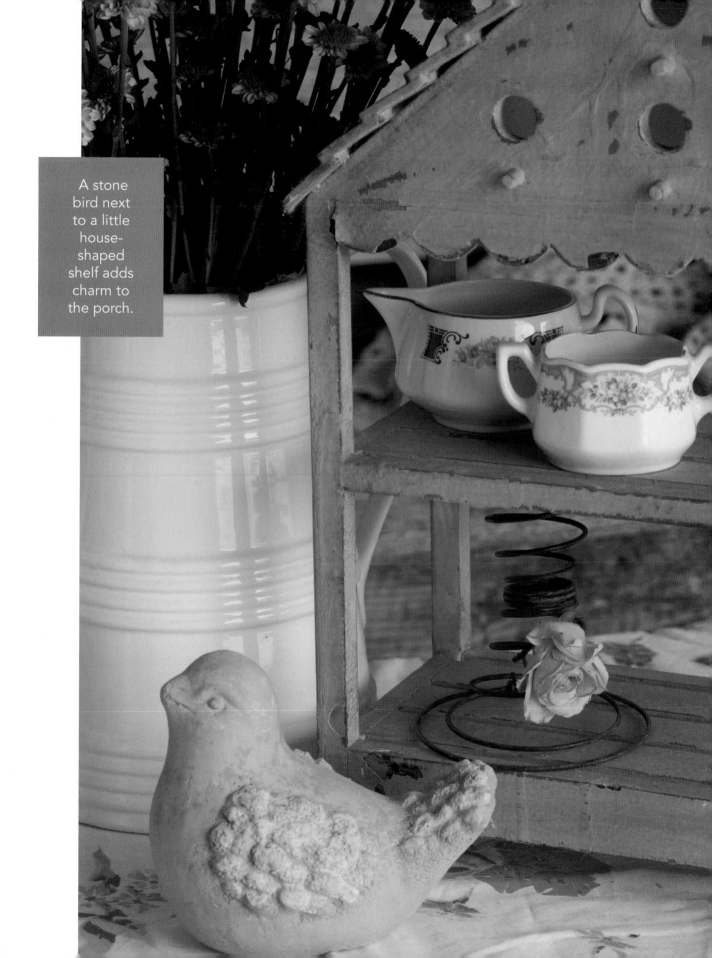

A stone bird next to a little house-shaped shelf adds charm to the porch.

20%. Twenty percent of $400 is $80, meaning the actual price you are paying is $480 plus tax. So you actually only saved $20, plus the tax on the $20. Considering the auction house is a drive for me, and I have to go at a time of day that often doesn't work for me, a $20 savings is not worth it. More and more you can bid online and by phone, so that is an option for you to consider.

5. Look over the item closely before bidding.

I preview online to see what items will be in the auction, and I do a close inspection before the auction to ensure there is no hidden damage or defects. Don't be afraid to walk around the room during the auction. Better safe than sorry, since once you win the bid, it's yours with no returns. If there is an obvious problem with the piece the auctioneer may point it out, but subtle problems are not often mentioned, since it is your responsibility to check the item over carefully. Buyer beware, so be safe or be sorry. If you want to bid online or by phone, call the auction house and ask for a condition report on the item.

6. Don't wave at your friend during the auction.

It is just best not to move your arms about during an auction unless you are actually bidding. The auctioneer is a master of knowing who is bidding and who isn't but still isn't a mind reader. If you must move your arm, or scratch your nose, avoid eye contact with the auctioneer, while doing so. He or she will know you are not bidding. If you are looking at the auctioneer, don't nod your head or move your arm about. I have seen that interpreted as a bid, and it can be confusing to the auctioneer. I just think it is more polite to not make the auctioneer work so hard; don't make them guess. Some auction houses may be less forgiving, and expect you to pay up on accidental bidding.

7. Set a maximum bid.

Before I start bidding, I have a figure in my mind of what I think the item should go for and what I am willing to pay. I make sure to factor in the buyers premium also. Once the bidding reaches my maximum, I stop, period. I have a fear that I will be caught up in the excitement and go crazy, so I limit myself. It's probably a good thing.

8. Know what will fit in your vehicle.

It is not unusual for me to end up with a large piece of furniture in my car. It happens more than I care to admit. I know what will fit and what won't. It's like a sixth sense, honed over many years of furniture buying. You will want to know if what you are buying will fit. If it won't fit, then you will need to consider the cost of delivery and roll that into the price. Most auction houses do not deliver, but they can usually recommend a good delivery service.

9. Don't be intimidated.

I used to look around the room and assume everyone there was much more knowledgeable than I was about antiques. At some point, I realized that most of the people attending the auctions are not experts. Many have some knowledge, but very few are actual experts. They are buying what they think they can sell in their shop. Sometimes I see items at the auction that are clearly reproductions. The auction houses often include consignment or estate pieces in with the regular antique auctions, so being able to tell the age of a piece is helpful. If you are unsure and want to know, ask someone who works at the auction house. They are usually happy to give you their opinion. If you want to determine the age of a dresser or chest, one of the best places to look is inside drawers and on the back. If it looks pristine and uniform, it is NOT an antique. Also check the dovetail joints. Are they uniform or non-uniform? If the dovetail joints are all exactly the same size, then the piece was machine made, making it "newer." If the joints are all a different size or shape, then it was handmade, placing it much earlier, 1800s or before, typically. Chairs can be examined from the bottom. The more you look at antiques, the more you will begin to know the antiques from the reproductions. You will get a feel for how something really old looks. The wood usually looks very old or new.

If you want to know what old stuff looks like, spend some time hanging out at an antique shop. Ask questions and examine the furniture. You will probably learn a good deal. If the shop owner was helpful, try to buy something there, even if it is something small. He just gave you a valuable, free lesson.

Silver is an easy way to add bling to a room.

10. Have fun.

I enjoy going to auctions. It is something fun for me to do. Sadly, I don't have as much time to attend and I have less and less need to attend for my own house. However, it really is an adventure, and I encourage you to go at least once. The people-watching alone is worth the trip. There is usually at least one dog in attendance dressed in a snazzy outfit. I'm not sure why that is. It's just one of life's mysteries. Some auction houses attract buyers wearing high heels, dressed to the nine's, carrying Yves St. Laurent bags, while others appear to bring in a rather sketchy crowd. Either way, I always have fun.

Craigslist

Here are my tips for buying on Craigslist, including my safety tips.

1. Call, don't email.

If there's a phone number in the ad, call, don't email. Callers are often given priority over emailers. And since many of the emailers are spammers, some sellers only respond to callers.

2. Contact the seller immediately!

If it is a fabulous piece, it will only be available for a few hours. I had a seller say he was holding an item for me, but that turned out to not be the case. Don't count on the seller holding it for you even if he says he will. The safest bet to go by and pick it up as soon as you can.

3. Ask for a phone number.

If the ad did not have a phone number be sure to ask for one. You may get lost and need directions, or you may need to cancel at the last minute.

4. Confirm your appointment.

You don't want the seller to forget you are coming. And if it is sold, you want to know before you leave the house. Once when confirming an appointment, I found out that the seller sold it even though he had promised it to me. If the location is a long drive, it's even more important to confirm.

5. Bring cash.

Since many sellers won't accept checks, especially on big-ticket items, it is always best to have cash with you. Bring smaller bills in case the seller will accept less.

6. Check out the item thoroughly.

Be sure to check the bottom, back, and sides. Look for damage and wear and tear. Make sure it is in acceptable condition. You will probably not be able to return it, if you notice something later.

7. Leave your fancy car at home.

If you show up in a very expensive car, don't expect the best price. Showing up in a Mercedes will not make the seller sympathetic to your budgetary issues. I don't recommend haggling to get a better price if you show up wearing Gucci either.

8. Ask for the best price.

See item 7. Assuming you are following rule number 7, there is probably some negotiating room. I usually ask, and when I ask, have always been offered a lower price. I don't ask for a better price if the asking price is already super low or if I can see the person needs the money. I also try to be very polite when I ask.

9. Don't point out all of the flaws.

Showing the seller what is wrong with the piece is not a good strategy to get a better price. Having worked in a furniture store, I can't tell you how annoying this is. Just ask if the price is the best one or if there is negotiating room on the price. The owner is probably aware of the defect and has already adjusted the price accordingly. A buyer that is nice will be given a better price than a buyer that comes off as critical.

10. Go with a friend.

If you feel uncomfortable going alone, ask a friend to go with you. If you can't find anyone to go with you, you can tell a friend when and where you will be, and ask her to call you at a certain time. If you don't answer, then she'll know where to send reinforcements.

11. Meet in a public place.

I have met people at their home, but trust your intuition and never take chances if you have an uneasy feeling about a location or a seller. When possible, it is safest to meet in a public location. If it is a piece of furniture, this may be difficult to arrange with the seller. Just use your best judgment.

Antique Stores

I used to avoid antique stores, since they seemed to be the most expensive places to buy from, but recently I have found some great deals at antique stores. Just keep location in mind. Fancy addresses have fancy prices, and valet parking at the antique store is a great tipoff that you'll be paying more than you ought to. Less fashionable parts of town have better prices. Antique malls can also be a nice place to shop. Just do your homework, so you can compare prices. The more educated you are, the better you will know your options, and what is a good price.

Resale/Thrift Stores

Thrift or resale shops are usually linked to a charity. They are stocked with items that were donated to them. The thrift stores that accept consignment items are the BEST ones. Because people don't often donate their nice things, the shops that handle consignment items have a better selection, and nicer things, but still have wonderful prices. Often finding the best places to buy requires going to the stores yourself or asking around.

Consignment Stores

Consignment stores are a mixed bag. Sometimes they have good stock and sometimes they don't, and prices can vary wildly. Definitely take a look in your area to see if you have any nearby. They are usually priced a bit higher than thrift stores, but they have nicer items. The other thing to keep in mind is that the price often goes down the longer the item has been there. Be sure to ask about their markdown policy.

eBay

eBay is a great place to find things, with a few caveats. Antique furniture seems ridiculously overpriced. Of course with the price of fuel, it just doesn't make sense to buy furniture on eBay if you then have to pay for shipping. I do not buy furniture on eBay, BUT I do buy a lot of other things on eBay. I recently wanted a toast rack. Have you ever looked for a toast rack? They are not easy to find. I didn't want to drive all over town looking for one, and probably come home empty-handed. I am careful about not buying anything too heavy on eBay because of the shipping cost. And if the item is not in the US, beware! I did this once, and after the sale, the seller pressured me to pay an additional fee for faster shipping. I paid the "blackmail" fee, and ended up paying a ridiculous sum for a Fortnum and Mason basket shipped from Great Britain. Now, I only buy small, lightweight items on eBay that are located in the US. Here is a list of things to consider when buying on eBay:

1. Know the shipping cost.

Make sure you know ahead of time what the shipping cost will be. It is usually listed, but if it isn't, send the seller a question requesting a shipping quote before you bid. Some sellers only charge for actual shipping costs, while others charge a handling fee. Sometimes the handling fees are too high. Make sure you know the total cost of shipping and handling before bidding.

2. Know the market value.

Having an idea ahead of time what the item should sell for is very helpful. If you don't know what the item would sell for in a store, then you don't know if you are overpaying.

3. Set your price limit.

Know the top price you are willing to pay ahead of time, and stick with it. This way you won't get caught up in the excitement of bidding.

4. Check seller feedback.

Verify that the seller has lots of feedback, and that it is at least 98% positive. I look for thousands of reviews, not just a handful.

5. Know where seller is located.

Know where the seller is shipping the item from, since you will be paying for that shipping. Are they in another country? Would you be able to reach them if you had an issue? Is the shipping cost going to be worth it? Personally, I have made the decision not to buy outside of the US.

6. Buyer beware.

Read the description carefully and assume nothing. Often you can't return these items. Even if you can, you will often be responsible for the cost of return shipping, and you will have the hassle of returning the item.

7. Ask questions.

Think of everything you might want to know before purchasing the item. If the description does not answer all of your questions, don't hesitate to send the seller any unanswered questions. Do this before bidding.

8. Verify smoke-free condition.

Make sure it is from a smoke-free home, unless a smoke smell isn't an issue for you. Many, if not most of the items on eBay, are from smoke-free homes, but still I would check. If the

seller has lots of positive feedback, you are probably safe. If you don't ask, and it doesn't specify, you may not be able to return it for smoke odor. Be safe and verify. Often it clearly states that in the description.

9. Verify pet-free condition.

Often items are from a pet-free environment, but not always. If you are allergic, make sure the item has not been exposed. Returns are no fun for anyone, and sometimes they are not accepted. Again if it doesn't specify, be sure to ask.

10. Know the shipping policy.

The bigger sellers have a shipping policy, meaning they state how often they ship. So if they ship on Saturdays, and you purchased on Tuesday, you can expect your item to ship the next Saturday. Delivery date will vary depending on how far you are from the shipping location. Also they often state who the carrier is and if tracking information will be provided. Be sure you understand how they operate before you bid. You don't want to be waiting a month for something you thought would arrive in a few days.

11. Know if insurance is included.

Some sellers will include insurance in their shipping fees while others do not. Be sure you know what you are paying for. If you do want insurance and it is not included, simply ask if you can add it. Conversely, if they include insurance and you don't want it, you can always ask for that fee to be removed.

12. Pay promptly.

It's just common courtesy to pay for an item as soon as you win the bid. I try to pay immediately. Don't leave the seller wondering if you will "make good." And if you need more incentive, they are rating you as a buyer. You want lots of positive feedback that other eBayers will see, whether you are buying or selling. Some sellers will only do business with buyers that have met a minimum rating.

13. Leave feedback.

After receiving the item, if satisfied, leave feedback for seller. The feedback is extremely important. This is how the seller proves she is reputable, so your rating is very important to her. If, however, you had a bad experience, please try to resolve it with the seller before you leave bad feedback. Bad feedback really hurts sellers. The reputable ones will usually go out of their way to make you happy. But if you don't tell them, they can't fix it.

Shopping at the Round Top Antique Show

It's hard to describe the Round Top Antique Show to someone who hasn't been. Someone asked if it was like a big flea market, and the answer is yes, and no. Yes it is like a flea market in that it there are many booths and lots of cool antiques there. But I would say no, in that it is much, much larger than any flea market I have ever been to. The first thing to keep in mind is that this is not just one location or venue, there are approximately seventy-five locations of shopping. Each location has many booths. The total number of vendors that show at Round Top is a staggering number and I am not sure anyone has a good count of the total. Suffice it to say, if you want it, it's probably there. The other thing that makes it not like a flea market is there is a large variety of the type of goods for sale. There is estate jewelry, antique sterling napkin holders, grain sacks, furniture, clothing, sculptures, and large architectural pieces. There are new items, vintage items, and antique items. They come from places all around the world including many from Europe. Some items are inexpensive, and some run into five digits.

Round Top Antique Week is one of my favorite times of the year. The shows happen once in the spring and once in the fall. The exact times vary from venue to venue, but most every location is open the first Saturday in April and the preceding week. It happens again the first Saturday in October and the preceding week. Many are open for a total of two weeks, although some, like Marburger, only open Tuesday–Saturday (the first of April) then again Tuesday–Saturday (the first of October.) Check out the current schedule at www.antiqueweekend.com.

The antiques stretch for miles and miles along Texas state highway 237. If you are coming from state highway 290, simply turn south onto 237, and you will come across venue after venue after venue for miles and miles. The complete map can be found at roundtop.com. You will think you died and went to antique/vintage/junk heaven. I get a lot of my goodies here.

There are many more locations in the area, but the bulk of the locations are on state highway 237.

So now you know where Round Top is and when it is, let's talk about preparing to go. You'll need a place to stay if you aren't local. The bad news is that this is a very rural area and there aren't any hotels around to speak of. Round Top prides itself on being the smallest incorporated city in Texas, but I'm not sure that's still true. (Let's just keep that to ourselves.) There are several bed and breakfast places nearby, but they fill up early. Check out www.antiqueweekend. com for a list of accommodations. I recommend booking as early as you can. There are a few motels nearby, several bed and breakfasts, and even some local homes that are available to rent during the show.

I like to go during the week, but if you decide to go on the weekend, here's what you need to know. It's crowded. And when I say it's crowded, I mean the cars inch along 237 and it can take 30 minutes to go a few miles. If you can, I recommend going during the week. If you must come on the weekend, save yourself the stress and come early.

Marburger Farm booth belonging to Paul and Suzanne Whitmire

The first thing to keep in mind is that you will probably not stay in the same location all day. You'll be going from place to place, so you will definitely need a car. The shopping stretches over ten miles of state highway 237, and in several towns, including Round Top, Warrenton, Carmine, Burton, La Grange, and Fayetteville. While you are at it, bring a large car so you'll have room for your purchases, or better yet, bring an SUV. Who knows, you might find that perfect piece of furniture that's just right.

You'll also need comfortable walking shoes. Leave the cute heels behind. There is a lot of walking, and most of the walking will be in fields, or on gravel, so walking shoes, hiking boots, or sneakers will be perfect. It will also be hot, and plan on rain. It doesn't always rain, but I would definitely be prepared for it. It doesn't usually last long, but you could get caught in a downpour. A hat and sunglasses are also recommended. You'll be outdoors mostly. I don't usually use sunscreen, but depending on where you shop, you might need it.

I also recommend bringing a backpack or a shopping cart or trolley for purchases. You may buy something heavy and be a distance from your car. A trolly or shopping cart is the best way to transport something heavy. If you don't have a trolley or shopping cart, then a backpack is better than nothing. If you buy something large and bulky, many vendors have a place where you can drive up to the booth to pick up the item. I also like to bring an insulated water bottle so I have cold water all day long.

Food is more widely available every year. There are a handful of restaurants that are permanent, but during antique week, you'll find many food trucks and food booths at most of the larger locations like Marburger and Blue Hills. The Compound always has good food too.

Now let's talk about what I like to buy at Round Top and where you can find these things for yourself. There are so many fabulous booths and locations, so I'm just going to cover a sampling here.

Here's what I like to do on my trips to the antique show.

Marburger Farm

Marburger is not the first, but it seems to be the best known. It's one of the largest locations and the vendors are curated. There are many places you can get the good stuff at the antique show, but some locations are hit or miss, while you're more likely to find the "good stuff"' at Marburger. If you love Farmhouse French, you'll love

Marburger Farm booth belonging to Gloria McDonald, *Winnie and Tulula's*

Marburger. Most places have free admission, but Marburger charges per person. You'll get a bracelet that includes admission for the duration of the show. There are food vendors at Marburger, but be prepared for long lines. You can get silver, dishes, gorgeous pillows, and furniture at Marburger. There are so many things you'll love here. I found the large pine table on my back porch at Marburger. They even delivered it to my farm, because everyone there is super nice.

Marburger Farm booth belonging to Julian Jay Yupcavage, *Pottsville Antiques*

The Compound

The Compound is one of the newer venues, and it's well worth your time to visit. The vendors are also curated here, but it's free admission. It has gorgeous buildings filled with fabulous goodies, some new, and some old. The Compound has air-conditioning in the main building, and that's important on hot days. I've found some wonderful architectural pieces at the Compound. The Compound is very close to Marburger Farms. The food trucks at the Compound are quite good. They have nice bathrooms, since I know you want to know.

Blue Hills

Blue Hills has a wonderful selection of items. I love shopping for bedding and pillows there. They also have antiques and many vintage items and furniture. You can have a meal at their sit down food court. This is where I found the toile bedding for my farm bedroom.

Bill Moore Antiques

This is a great place to find vintage bottles, grain sacks, and scales. It's a big warehouse, so it's not styled like the booths at Marburger, but has a lot to choose from. This is where I found my vintage bottles and linens.

Old Depot Vintage Market

We always like to stop in at The Depot. If you are looking for monogrammed pillows or hide rugs, they have a good selection. This is one of the smaller venues, so it's rarely crowded except on the weekends. I found several of the hide rugs here. Some of the shopping is indoors, and there's a real bathroom here.

Cole's Antique Show

My friend Caroline always loves to go to Cole's. She always finds the best vintage jewelry here. There are a lot of vendors that sell vintage dishes here. It's air-conditioned, and there are food trucks nearby. If you are feeling droopy due to the heat, come inside Cole's and shop.

Clutter

Clutter is one of those places we always have to go visit. It's full of gorgeous vintage dishes. I don't always buy something there, but I always want to. If you are a dish collector, you'll want to check it out.

Excess

Excess has lots of large architectural pieces. You'll also find furniture here, and some very large and unique pieces at that. It's always worth the trip walking through here, because the pieces are all so unique. If you are looking for a large one-of-a-kind statement piece, try Excess.

Marburger Farm booth by Allison Watts

Warrenton Field

There's a little bit of everything in Warrenton. The fields stretch on and on and on. There are tents as far as the eye can see. There are a few places I want to suggest to you. There's a place near Excess that makes the most amazing lamps from salvaged pieces. I bought a lamp and wish I had more. I can't remember his name, but his lamps were amazing. The other vendor is Hans. Well, I don't know his last name, but he has Mora clocks, some stunning French furniture, and gorgeous baskets. I like just about everything he sells.

CHAPTER 6: FOUND OBJECTS & COLLECTING

Found Objects

Want to add instant charm to your room? If you want your home to feel warm, unique, and magazine worthy, one of the best ways is to include vintage or antique pieces in your home. I'm amazed what a difference they make in a room. Old things are so fascinating to me. Sometimes I feel like they should be in a museum, but instead, I get to hold and touch them. I have an original Louis Felipe mirror from pre-1850 France. I have a few other pieces from the 1800s as well. I wonder who that mirror saw before me.

Antique items are defined as things over 100 years old. Vintage refers to items over 20 years old, but not quite 100 years old. I'm going to be discussing them together as one group of things. They are, in a word, old. I like to see a mix of old and new in a room. The new things give the room life, and the old things give it character. A room full of only new things seems off to me. It's difficult to explain; a room with only new things seems to lack soul.

I want to see something unusual, something I can't just go to the mall and buy.

Using hanging hardware for doors instead of traditional hinges adds farmhouse style to a room.

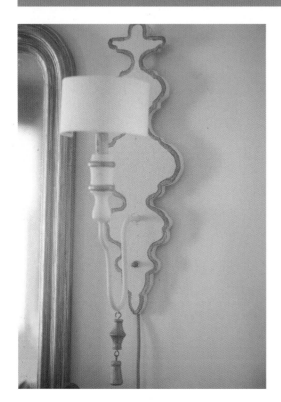

It is almost impossible to find new pieces with the character of old pieces.

Ceiling tiles are a great way to add instant vintage style to a wall.

You can even use vintage or antique materials when building your home. We added antique corbels and the salvaged board to make a shelf in our hallway. A shelf like this could be easily added to most any home.

Another way we incorporated antique materials was to use an old iron fence post as a newel post for the stairs.

Right: A shelf like this one could be added to just about any home.

Old iron shelves like these shown are not only attractive, but provide extra storage space.

Salvaged beadboard made for a unique one-of-a-kind porch ceiling.

Clocks

Many old clocks are beautiful works of art. I don't actually use them to tell time, but you could. They add a beautiful, historical feel to the room.

Seltzer Bottles

Seltzer bottles are increasing in popularity, and look great when displayed in a bar area, or when collected and displayed together.

Statues

Statues are often very elegant. It's a way to add three-dimensional art to a room. I love to stare at them, wondering who posed for the artist, and too wondering what her life was like. They sometimes even seem to have a personality.

Trophies

Trophies, like statues and clocks, can be beautiful works of art with a history. They are usually personalized with the name of the award, the recipient name, or names and the date. My "best developed man" trophy is truly my favorite because who doesn't love a well-developed man?

Books

Old books are just as fascinating, but are even more versatile. They can be stacked in a bookcase or used as a riser beneath other objects. I use them all over the house.

Bottles

Bottles look great most anywhere. They come in a variety of sizes, so you can usually find the size you need, if you know where to look.

Linens

Old linens are a work of art. Some have lace, some are monogrammed, and still others are decorated with hand-stitching. They are wonderful used as table runner, made into a pillowcase, or just stacked in a cabinet.

Baskets

Baskets, especially vintage ones, can be a work of art, and they, too, are very versatile. They can be very interesting on their own, but also provide storage for many different types of items.

Hats

Old hats are intriguing to me because they too make me wonder about who wore them. What did the person look like? Where did she live? What was her life like? A hat is very interesting also because it seems so personal.

Paintings

Paintings are fun to display since they seem personal—meaning someone created it. They can be pricey, so I don't have too many. I especially love portraits. Is it just me? I have a fascination with people, especially people who are long gone.

Silver

Vintage silver can be very beautiful. No matter what your taste is, there are so many different patterns available, there are probably one or two that will appeal to you. The best part about vintage silverware is that you can actually use it, not just look at it. I love the bling of the silver and the craftsmanship.

Dishes

Vintage dishes, like vintage silver, come in many, many different patterns. You can find them in about any color or pattern you prefer. When displaying or using the dishes, you can stick to a matched set or mix and match.

A hat is interesting because it seems so personal.

Displaying Collections

Only collect what you love. I personally would never buy art as an investment. Some people do make money selling artwork, but from what I hear, it is rare. Why waste time collecting something you don't like if you probably won't make money on it? Collect what has meaning to you. Most people don't make money when they sell their collections. Sure you hear about the odd person here or there who makes a million dollars on something they thought was worthless, but that is the exception to the rule.

I think collections are fun, and even if you collect the same thing as someone else, your collection will be unique to you. So if you want to start a collection, think of what you like, and what you can afford to collect. Then buy only the best of that item. I collect dishes. At first I wasn't picky. I picked up many dishes at garage sales that I didn't really like that much, but they were cheap. Then I inherited a lot of dishes. I had literally hundreds of dishes. I had no idea how much I had, I just knew it was too much. And so I did the right thing, I gave a lot away. I kept the best ones, but gave away the ones that I didn't really care about. That was at least half of the collection. I even sold a few. My collection became better, more refined—

more of a collection and less of a warehouse. For the most part, I kept the dishes made in the USA, France, Portugal, England, and Italy.

This smaller collection made more sense to me. It's not about having a lot of something, but about having a grouping of things, with a common theme, that makes you smile.

Once you begin collecting, the next issue is how to display it. You could store it in boxes, in the attic or basement, but my philosophy is what is the point of having a collection if you can't or don't display it? If it is in a box, you will forget about it and not enjoy it. I don't enjoy knowing I have a collection of hand-painted French dishes, I enjoy touching them, seeing them, and using them.

Collections can sometimes grow out of hand and overwhelm a room. So, how can they be displayed beautifully in a room? One of the best ways to display a rather large collection is in a bookcase, in glass-front cabinets, or in a cupboard.

For smaller collections, you will have many more options. For displaying linens or towels, try using a vintage wooden ladder.

Smaller collections can be often be organized into a tray. They can also be grouped together on a desktop, or on a chest, organized on a bookcase, or inside a cabinet.

Personally, I prefer my collections to look neat and orderly. If you have a collection of small items sitting on a desktop, it can look cluttered and jumbled. Small things display better if they are all contained into a cupboard or cabinet.

CHAPTER 7: ANTIQUE FURNITURE

Antiques have a past and a history; they are the keepers of secrets. Yes, they are usually imperfect, with a scratch here and a dent there, but slight signs of age make them so much more appealing to me. They usually have a patina impossible to replicate, especially on painted pieces. New furniture just doesn't have the detail, and usually isn't as well built as antique furniture. Hand carved detail is becoming a thing of the past. I also am a bit of a romantic and like to think about who owned the furniture, how the owners used the furniture, and what the original owners were like. Well-made furniture seems to be more and more a thing of the past. Now there is competition to make furniture cheaper and cheaper, so the focus is no longer on craftsmanship, but on profit margin. So furniture is made in a much more simple style, without hand carving or much of an eye to detail. When I find a manufacturer that does include those beautiful details, the cost of the furniture is often very, very high.

Manufacturers are competing on price with cheaply-made imported furniture. That is a recipe for cheap, mass-produced, unimaginative furniture. If a craftsman spends too much time on a chair, he can't sell it, because the buyer can go down the street to buy a much cheaper model. The bottom line is that most people are not willing to pay for good craftsmanship any more. More and more, I turn to vintage and antique furniture. Happily (for me) the young people in Europe are selling family heirlooms to buy new cheap furniture. They think the old furniture isn't in step with modern life. Very sad for them, but happy for those of us looking to buy the old furniture.

I buy up all I can. Hand-carved walnut wood makes my heart go pitter-patter. Yes, often these pieces need to be refreshed. The chairs need new upholstery, or the seat bottoms are broken. If I can do the repair or have it done without a ridiculous expense, I go for it.

Here are some things to keep in mind when buying antique furniture:

FURNITURE BUYING CHECKLIST

1. Look the piece over for previous damage and repairs, especially bad repair jobs.

    Any repair job will reduce the value of the piece, a poor repair much more so than a professional one. A previous repair will not keep me from buying a piece, it just depends on how obvious the repair is.

2. Check the back and bottom.

3. Does the piece look really dirty on the bottom and back?

   Often repair work can only be seen on the back or bottom. These are places that give hints at the age of the piece. Dirt and wear indicate a much older piece. Clean, smooth, straight areas indicate something much newer.

4. Open drawers, open doors, sit in chairs, try latches.

   You want to check to be sure drawers open easily. Chairs need to be able to hold the weight of people sitting in them. Latches, pulls, and handles should be sound.

5. Check to see if any locks have the keys that go with them.

   It is nice to get the key to a piece, but again I have bought pieces missing the key.

6. Ask for any information the owner has about the piece.

   Sometimes they can tell you about the history of the piece, but most of the time they don't know. Still, if you don't ask, you probably won't get any information.

7. Inspect the joints on the drawers.

   Are the drawer joints dovetail? If not, then the piece is probably new. Are the dovetail joints uniform? Uniform joints mean the piece is probably machine made and newer. Non-uniform joints appear on handmade and older pieces.

8. Are there any screws in the piece?

   Metal screws indicate a newer piece, but the screw could just be a repair.

9. Do the nails look new or very old?

   Obviously the older the nails look, the older the piece is.

10. Has the hardware or anything else on the piece been replaced?

    If it has been replaced, that will probably affect the value, but it wouldn't necessarily keep me from buying it. Missing hardware can often be replaced too.

11. Does the piece appear handmade or machine made?

    How uniform is it? To answer this question, you will need to see the bottom and the back of the piece. I once bought a table that looked old, but I didn't realize how old it was until I saw the bottom of the table. It had been cut by hand. A chair I bought has one leg noticeably more narrow than the others. It is clearly made by hand. The more uniform and neat the piece, the newer it probably is.

12. Is the seller asking a reasonable price?

Answering this question requires a bit of research. What is the going rate for similar items in your area? Prices can vary greatly by geographical areas. Large cities often are known for having higher prices, but even within a city, prices can vary depending on street and neighborhood. Find out what you could buy a similar piece for somewhere else.

13. Is there any room to negotiate a better price?

14. If the owner won't come down on the price, will he deliver for free?

15. If it is a mirror, is the edge of the glass (on the back side) smooth or jagged?

16. If it is a mirror, how is the glass held in place?

17. Are all of the surfaces very uniform and machine finished?

Anything that makes the furniture look like it was made by hand versus machinery is going to date the piece older.

18. Is the piece a one-of-a-kind?

If this piece is unusual, then it will be difficult to determine what it "should" sell for. And if you are crazy in love with it, then maybe it is worth paying more for this piece, rather than waiting to find a cheaper version somewhere else. I will pay a lot extra for a very special piece. I used to be very budget conscious, and just wouldn't pay much of a premium for a special piece. As I have gotten older, I appreciate those unusual pieces a lot more.

Buying used furniture is very different from buying new furniture. For new furniture, I basically check to make sure I like the look, the fabric is what I wanted, and also make sure it is comfortable. Buying used furniture is completely different. If you buy a new settee and it breaks a month after you buy it, often there is a warranty in place. At least there was when mine broke during a teeny-bopper slumber party at my house. (Don't ask.) They sent me a new one, post haste.

If you buy used furniture, don't expect to get your money back or even any sympathy if it breaks or you change your mind. It is pretty much buyer beware. Car and home sellers may have to disclose defects, but there is no such requirement on furniture, so far as I know. The good news is that old furniture tends to be more solid and sturdy. The problem with breakage comes from the fact that the furniture is old, and can have loose joints, torn fabric, dents, scratches, chips, gouges, and major repairs. To really inspect the piece, you need to turn it over and look at the bottom. Check for previous repairs. One time, I saw a chair leg that had broken off completely then was bolted back together in the most Frankenstein-like fashion; it was a bit creepy. The leg wasn't even straight any more, but was bent in an awkward, painful-looking way. Look it over very carefully. Ask questions of the seller. Ask if the seller knows of any specific damage. Antique dealers tend to be an honest bunch. If you ask, and they know there is a problem, usually they will tell you.

If I am considering buying a chair, I sit in it, and notice what happens next, hopefully . . . nothing. Does it creak, when I sit in it? Does it feel like it is about to give way? Gently push the back of the chair forward and back. Are the joints loose? My daughter was sitting in an antique chair I put in her room when she was a teenager. Over time, it began to give way, and the legs began to spread a bit more each day. An adult would have realized that the chair could no longer be trusted in its present condition and stopped using it. Being a teenager, she continued to use it, until one day, SPLAT the chair broke apart from the seat, and she toppled to the floor. I was able to repair it later, but eventually it broke again. Here is a list of signs I look for that tell me to walk away from an antique piece of furniture.

Deal Breakers

1. Wobbly legs

2. Major obvious repairs

3. A chair that I'm afraid to sit in

4. Legs that have been previously broken and glued back together

5. Smoke odor

6. Ridiculously high price

7. Too big for the space

Now that we have discussed furniture warning signs 101, let's talk about some problems you might notice that are not a big deal. Either they are fixable, or just something that isn't going to bother you long-term. Remember the piece can almost always be painted. If you don't like the paint or stain, that is one of the easiest fixes. Upholstery and slip covering are a bit more complicated.

While we are talking about what to look for in antique furniture, let's talk about what is considered normal wear. Antiques, by definition, are over one hundred years old. Most things over a hundred years old that have been used consistently will show some wear and age. For antique chair or table, that means there will be scratches. There might be a deep scratch, or

even a gouge. You will need to decide what is acceptable damage and wear, and what is not. Repairs will affect value also, but again, I wouldn't buy the piece based on its resale value, but whether or not the piece appeals to you. For example, the chair I mentioned that broke in my daughter's room is hand-carved and a real beauty. Some people would have said it wasn't worth keeping and thrown it out. I repaired it by screwing the legs to the seat. It isn't the best repair, but it became usable again.

On the other hand, there are plenty of antiques worth loads of money that I just find ugly, and wouldn't buy for any reason. Some readers told me not to paint my chair because it would affect the value. If it were a rare antique, yes they are absolutely correct. But for a non-valuable antique, updating it makes its appeal much broader, often increasing its value. Value is based on what people are willing to pay for something. If the piece appears dated, even if in original condition, few people will want it, and thus it has little market value. (There are exceptions to this rule of course.) I wouldn't forgo painting something just because it is

old. It really depends on how I feel about the piece. If you suspect your antique furniture is valuable, please consult with an appraiser before doing anything to the piece.

Okay Problems

This is a list of problems that would not keep me from buying a piece of furniture, and I'll show you how to make some of these repairs in later chapters.

1. Ugly upholstery
   (FIX: Re-upholstery)

2. Broken caned seat
   (FIX: Repair caning or make new seat)

3. Ugly paint color
   (FIX: Paint)

4. Ugly wood stain
   (FIX: Paint or refinish)

5. Missing hardware
   (FIX: Replace hardware)

6. Torn leather
   (FIX: Re-upholster)

7. Lost key
   (FIX: Don't lock it)

8. Light scratches and dents
   (FIX: Ignore)

9. Worm holes
   (FIX: Ignore, unless it is an active infestation. How do you tell? Put a white paper or sheet under the furniture and check it a few days later. If there are bits of insects there or fresh sawdust, you'll need to call an expert to fumigate the piece. I'm not sure how to check before you buy the piece.)

CHAPTER 8: HOW TO PAINT AND DISTRESS FURNITURE

I often buy sad, discarded furniture that the owner no longer wants. These pieces often need paint, re-upholstery, or a new seat. I will take about anything with good bones. I draw the line at wobbly or obviously broken furniture, but otherwise am not too picky . . . so long as it is French.

If the piece has good bones, but is covered in a less than stellar fabric, I will send it off with fabric to be recovered. Often that is all that is needed to make a chair right as rain. Some people do this step themselves, and I applaud them for it, but I will happily pay. There are some things that just aren't worth losing your sanity for, and upholstery is one of them, at least for me.

Now this chair was a trifecta of junk. The seat was completely broken, the stain was dark and shiny, and the cushion was undersized for the seat. I knew that with a new seat, paint, and a new cushion, this piece would shine. I don't know how to re-cane furniture, but I do know how to use a saw. Here's how I redid my chair:

Repairing the Seat

1. Measure seat and cut a piece of newspaper to fit it.

2. Then place newspaper on seat to fine tune the size, cutting around the arm supports.

3. Trim newspaper to make slightly bigger than the caned part of the seat, but not much bigger.

   It needs to reach the sturdy wood part of the seat so that the wood frame supports the new seat. Make sure to allow a lot of room for chair arms if there are any. This is accomplished by trimming just a bit at a time, but be sure not to overtrim. After a few minutes, it should fit the chair seat pretty closely. This newspaper is now your pattern.

4. Place the newspaper pattern on very thin plywood and trace around it with a pencil.

5. Remove the paper after the image is traced onto the plywood.

6. Using a jigsaw, cut along the lines.

7. Place new piece on your chair.

   Now you have a new support for your seat. This piece sits on top of the chair seat and supports the weight of a person. I am not opposed to repairing the seats,

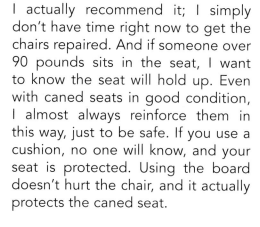

I actually recommend it; I simply don't have time right now to get the chairs repaired. And if someone over 90 pounds sits in the seat, I want to know the seat will hold up. Even with caned seats in good condition, I almost always reinforce them in this way, just to be safe. If you use a cushion, no one will know, and your seat is protected. Using the board doesn't hurt the chair, and it actually protects the caned seat.

Paint the Chair

This technique requires that you use a chalk-based paint. If you haven't heard of it before, you might be wondering why this paint is preferred over latex. If you want to distress the piece by sanding it, then the latex paint must cure for days before distressing. If you try to distress it as soon as it dries, the paint ends up peeling off, which is not the look you want. Also if you are using latex paint, if you paint over a previously unpainted surface, you really should prime the piece first. Chalk-based paint does not require that. And if your piece has been waxed, the wax must be removed before you paint with latex paint, but not with chalk-based paint. Also, chalk-based paint is flat, which is the look most people want; however, you can buy latex paint in a flat finish.

These directions are for use with chalk-based paint. These directions are not for use with latex- or oil-based paint. If you prefer to make your own, you can do that as well. Mix about ¼ cup of warm water with three tablespoons of calcium carbonate powder and stir until the calcium carbonate is dissolved. Calcium carbonate can be purchased at a health food store or ordered from Amazon.com. Some people use plaster of Paris or unsanded grout instead of calcium carbonate. I did not have good results with plaster of Paris. As for using unsanded grout, I haven't tried that option yet. Next, mix in one cup of latex paint. Once it is fully incorporated, use paint as you would latex paint; however, no sanding or priming is required.

1. Clean the chair with a damp cloth. It's important, even when using chalk-based paint to begin with a clean surface.

2. Check to see if your furniture has been previously painted with lead-based paint. If the piece was made before 1978, and it is painted, assume the paint contains lead. You can also purchase a lead test kit to ascertain if your painted piece was painted with lead-based paint.

3. If you suspect your piece has lead-based paint on it, please check with the EPA on the best way to address the potential health hazards. Addressing health issues is beyond the scope of this book, but please do your research and be safe. Now assuming you are not working with lead-based paint, proceed . . .

4. If the piece has previously been painted and the paint is not lead-based, check it for loose paint. Any loose paint will need to be removed, but it usually comes off with sandpaper or a brush.

5. Open can of chalk-based paint and stir, or you can use your own homemade chalky paint.

6. For this chair, I used paint from Southern Honey, color Stanley. Apply the first coat of paint, like you would using latex paint.

7. Allow the paint to dry in between coats of paint.

8. Apply a second coat of paint. In most cases, two coats of paint will be sufficient. Apply a third only if needed.

Distress the Chair

Some people will not want to distress the paint finish, and that is totally up to you. If you do desire to add an antiqued finish, here is how you can do it. If you choose not to distress the paint finish, you will still need to add a coat of clear wax to protect the finish.

1. If you are new to this technique, I suggest you use a practice board first. A practice board is simply an extra piece of wood that you can paint, wax, and distress to see if you are happy with your paint color, distressing, and wax technique. If you don't like how it looks, keep practicing until you find a technique that gives you the desired effect.

2. Lightly sand in areas that might have shown natural wear, like corners that might have knocked against a wall, arms that might have been used repeatedly. Oversanding or sanding in places that would not have shown wear will make it obvious this piece has been artificially distressed.

3. Wipe away the loose sawdust from the piece.

4. Select a wax you will use to finish the piece. If the paint is not too light, you can use an antiquing wax, meaning a brownish wax. If you do not want to use wax to antique the finish or if the piece is white, I suggest you use a clear wax. I used Southern Honey wax for the clear wax. I recommend using a wax brush. If you use  a cloth to apply the wax, you will waste a lot of wax. For antiquing wax, my current favorite is Howard Wax™ in Walnut. If you use tinted antiquing wax, keep in mind that this wax is brown, so it will change the look of the paint, making it darker and more yellow. Test the wax in an inconspicuous spot to ensure you like the effect. One thing you can do if you are concerned the wax will be too dark is to do a first coat of wax with clear wax. Then apply a coat of tinted wax. If you don't like the tinted wax, it will be much easier to remove if there is a clear coat of wax underneath. The darker wax can be removed to some extent by buffing with a cloth. If you want to remove more, then use sandpaper.

5. Apply the wax by dabbing a stiff bristled brush into the wax can, and then brushing it on your piece. For areas with hand carving, you'll need to use a jabbing motion to get the wax into the deep recesses.

6. Once you have applied the wax to an area the size of two pieces of bread, use a soft cloth to remove the excess wax and buff the area.

7. Continue until you finish waxing and buffing the entire piece. I have used this technique for years on many pieces of furniture. I used the very same technique on this next chair. The chair had been broken but I couldn't stand to part with it. I set it on top of my cabinet, but then one day decided to attempt a repair. I added some screws to the legs, so that the chair could be used again. Then I decided some paint would make it even lovelier. I not only painted the wood, but also changed the fabric seat on this chair.

I've even used the same technique on these mirrors. I added an extra layer of dry brushed paint to get the shade just right.

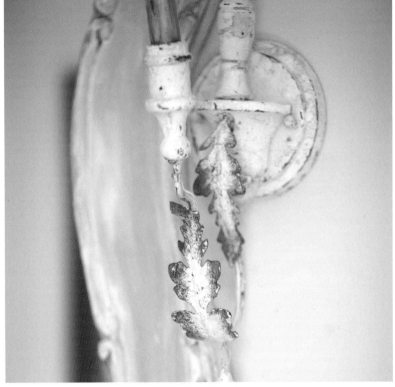

Detail on painted mirror

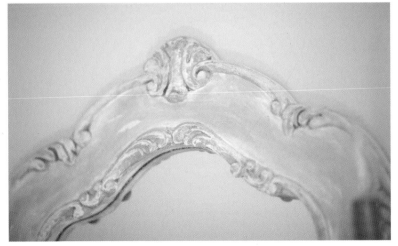

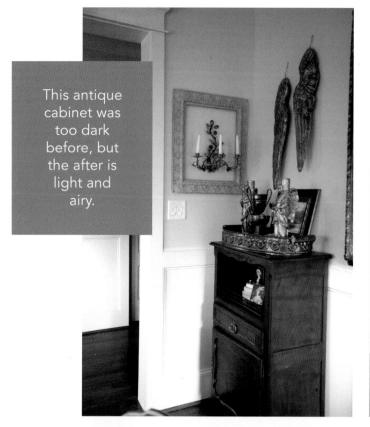

This antique cabinet was too dark before, but the after is light and airy.

CHAPTER 9 : MAKING A LONG DROP BEDSPREAD

I have been asked many times how I made my long drop bedspread, so I am including the instructions in the book. These instructions are for a queen-size bedspread with a thirty-inch drop length. You can use the instructions to make a bedspread for a twin, double, or king-size bed, if you modify the instructions to accommodate the bed size. If your bed has a different drop, then modify the directions accordingly. Make sure you have all of your supplies before beginning the project.

You will need:

- 2 (9 feet × 12 feet) drop cloths
- 1 spool of off-white thread
- 1 ruffler*
- 1 box of pins
- Iron and ironing board
- 2 (26-inch) euro pillow inserts

* You can instead use dark thread and a hand-sewing needle.

Before you begin, do yourself a favor and set up your ironing board near your sewing machine. You'll be using it quite a bit, and it will be handy to have it nearby.

1. Select drop cloth.
    - You will need two (9 feet × 12 feet) dropcloths. That's about $40! I used 10-ounce drop cloths from the Blue Hawk brand. I like the color of the Blue Hawk brand. Be careful not to purchase drop cloth that is too gray, or you won't like the results. You are looking for a dropcloth that is close to an oatmeal color.

2. Wash fabric.
    - The first thing you need to do is to wash and dry your fabric. The reason you should do this first is so that any fabric shrinking occurs before you begin sewing. Otherwise you could end up with an awful surprise—a bedspread that doesn't quite reach the floor.

- You will probably need to wash each drop cloth one at a time in your washing machine. It's preferable to pull them out of the dryer very slightly damp to reduce wrinkling.

3. Press fabric.

   After washing and drying the fabric, you will need to use your iron to press the fabric. You can't measure it properly when it's seriously wrinkled, which it probably will be when it comes out of the dryer. This is going to take a little bit of a time, but it is worth doing. If you take the fabric out while it is slightly damp, you can usually flatten it fairly easily with your hands to minimize the wrinkles.

4. Measure and cut drop cloth fabric for bedspread top. (Piece A)

   - Stretch out your fabric. If you don't have a big island, I would work on the floor. You are going to need a lot of space. As you spread out the fabric, you'll notice there are seams all along the edges of the drop cloth and smack dab in the middle.

   - Trim the seams along the top and bottom of each drop cloth as shown in the diagrams Drop Cloth 1 and Drop Cloth 2. When trimming, get as close to the seams as you can.

   - You need a piece 87 inches long by 61 inches wide for the top of the bedspread. It's important that you plan out how you will cut your fabric so you have enough.

   - Follow the layout shown in the diagram Drop Cloth 1. I measure with my yardstick, then mark the underside of the fabric in pencil.

DROP CLOTH SEAMS

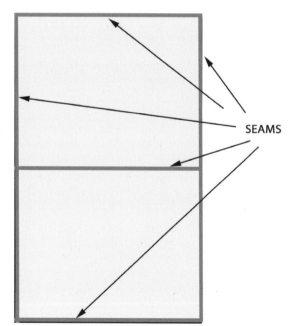

SEAMS

DROP CLOTH SEAMS

Trim top and bottom seams

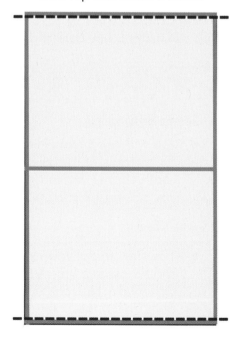

When you are using drop cloth, both sides are the same, so in this case, there is no "wrong side." Use the diagram to see where you should mark and cut the fabric for the top of the bedspread, piece A.

- After marking the fabric, cut along the lines you just marked. You will have a seam on one end after the fabric is cut. That will be the top or head of the bedspread.

5. **Now we are going to cut the fabric that we will use for the sides, or the drop.** Measure and cut the ruffle B1 from Drop Cloth 1 as shown in the top diagram. It should be the entire width of the fabric (approximately 9 feet) and 32½ inches tall.

6. **After you cut piece B1, set aside Drop Cloth 1.** Don't worry about the C, D, E, and F pieces just yet—we'll get to them later. Get Drop Cloth 2. The top and bottom hem should have already been cut off in step 4. Now measure and cut the remaining four pieces of the side ruffle: B2, B3, B4, and B5. They should all be the width of the drop cloth (9 feet) and 32½ inches tall.

7. **Sew the short side of B1 to the short side of B2.** Note that since we are working with drop cloth, it doesn't matter for this first seam which sides you designate as the "right sides," but after you do the first seam, make sure you sew the subsequent pieces so that all the seams are on the same side. Once you have sewn B1 to B2, sew the short side of B2 to the short side of B3, the short side of B3 to the short side of B4, and finally the short side of B4 to the short side of B5.

DROP CLOTH 1 (9 x 12)

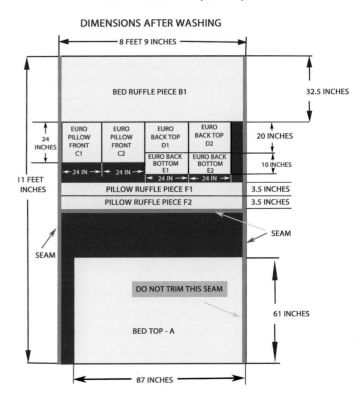

DROP CLOTH 2 (9 x 12)

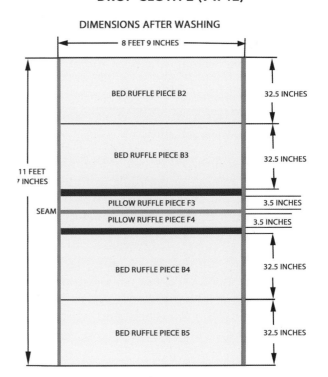

8. Now you should have one long piece of "B" fabric as seen in the diagram Bedspread Piece "B." Use your iron to press open all of the seams.

9. Next, fold the fabric over ½ inch along the long length of the B. Press the entire length of the piece of fabric for your bedspread ruffle. Fold over ½ inch again on the same side, and press again.

10. Pin the folds in place, then hem with the sewing machine. When you finish, you should have one very long piece of fabric, about 45 feet long, with the hem on one of the long sides. Remember that the fabric has probably shrunk, so it won't be exactly 45 feet. The hem will be for the bottom of the bedspread ruffle.

11. Next we'll ruffle the ruffle. You can do that by hand or by using the ruffler on your machine. There are instructions for both. If you are using a ruffler, skip down to step #33.

BEDSPREAD PIECE "B"

B1	B2	B3	B4	B5

← APPROXIMATELY 45 FT →

HEMMING RUFFLE

Ruffling by Hand

12. This bedspread has split corners. This is important for beds with a footboard. Over the next several steps, the ruffle will be cut into three pieces, one ruffle for the foot of the bed and one for each side of the bed. We are also going to gather the ruffles. I highly, highly recommend using a ruffler, which is an attachment for your sewing machine. If you don't have a ruffler, or just don't want to use one, then you can do the ruffling by hand. It's a lot more work though and much more frustrating.

13. First measure 120 inches of the ruffle. Cut off this section of the ruffle from the main ruffle. It will become the ruffle that will go at the foot of the bed as seen in bed ruffle diagram. (See Placement of First Ruffle).

14. For each short end of this piece, fold over ½ inch and press it. Fold them over another ½ inch and press again. Pin and sew the hem on each end. These are the sides of the ruffle. Remove pins. The

PLACEMENT OF FIRST RUFFLE

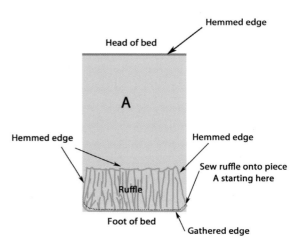

Head of bed

Hemmed edge

A

Hemmed edge

Hemmed edge

Sew ruffle onto piece A starting here

Ruffle

Foot of bed

Gathered edge

footer ruffle should now have a hem on the bottom and both sides as seen in Bed Ruffle Hems diagram.

15. Take your black thread and measure about 63 inches of thread. Cut it, then tie a sturdy knot on the end. Thread your needle. Do a running stitch along the top edge (not the hemmed end) about ½ inch from the top of the bed ruffle as shown in Bed Ruffle Hem diagram. The running stitch is a stitch consisting of a line of small even stitches that run in and out through the cloth without overlapping. Each stitch should be about ½ inch. When you are finished stitching, tie a knot at the end of the thread. The thread is shorter than the ruffle fabric. When you tie the knot, the ruffle will be gathered.

16. Once you have finished the running stitch, place piece A on your bed with the hemmed edge at the head of the bed as shown in diagram Placement of First Ruffle. The best looking side of the hem should be facing up. Place the footboard ruffle (Ruffle 1) along the foot of your bed, right side down as shown in diagram Placement of First Ruffle on page 122. Place the unfinished edge of the ruffle (where your black thread is) on top of the unfinished edge of piece A. Note: The ruffle should be lying on top of your bed, not hanging off the foot or side of your bed.

BED RUFFLE HEMS

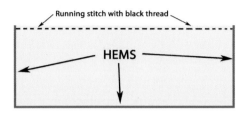

17. Spread out the ruffle, making the gathers as even as possible. Pin it in place, making sure to curve around the corners of the foot of the bed as shown in the Placement of First Ruffle diagram.

18. Sew the ruffle onto piece A, starting on the side indicated in the diagram with a ½-inch seam allowance. When sewing, make sure the ruffle is on top (right side down) rather than piece A. Remove pins.

19. Measure the length of the remaining piece B, along the long end. It should be approximately 35 feet long, possibly shorter due to shrinking. Measure to the halfway point, about 200 inches. Cut piece B at the halfway point, completely in half so that you have two pieces, with each piece being about 200 inches long. Remember, they might be a bit less than 200 inches due to shrinking. These two pieces are the ruffles for the sides of the bedspread (second and third ruffle).

20. Next, you'll need to hem the short ends of the side ruffles. One piece should already have a hem on one side, so you can ignore that one. For the sides that do not have a hem, press each end over ½ inch. Pin and sew the hem. Remove pins. Do this for the

short ends of each side ruffle (Ruffles 2 and 3). Each ruffle should have a hem on each short side and the bottom side as seen in the Bed Ruffle Hem diagram.

21. Just as you attached a ruffle to the foot of the bedspread, we will repeat the process for each side.

22. Place bedspread back on the bed, right side up. Make sure the ruffle for the foot of the bed that is already attached on top of the bed rather than hanging down, as shown in Placement of First Ruffle diagram.

PLACEMENT OF SECOND RUFFLE

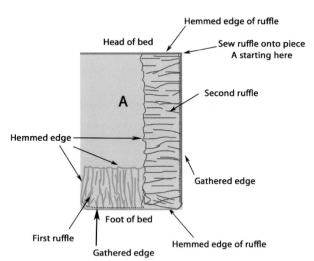

23. Take your black thread and measure about 90 inches of thread. Cut it, then tie a sturdy knot at the end. Thread your needle. Do a running stitch along the top edge (not the hemmed end) about ½ inch from the top of one of the B pieces. See Bed Ruffle diagram on page 123. This is now Ruffle 2. Each stitch should be about ½ inch. When you are finished stitching, tie a knot at the end of the thread. The thread is shorter than the ruffle fabric. When you tie the knot, the ruffle will be gathered.

24. Once you have done the running stitch, place the first side ruffle along the right side of your bed, as shown in diagram Placement of Second Ruffle. Place the unfinished edge of the ruffle on top of the unfinished edge of piece A. The ruffle should be lying on top of your bed, not hanging off the side of your bed. Ruffle should be oriented with right side down.

25. Spread out the ruffle, making the gathers as even as possible. Pin it in place, making sure to curve around the corner of the foot of the bed as shown in the diagram. This second ruffle should overlap the attached footboard ruffle by about 3 inches on the corner. Refer to the Ruffle Overlap image. The overlap should be at least 1 inch, and no more than 3 inches.

26. Sew Ruffle 2 on, starting at the head of the bed as shown, with a ½ inch seam allowance. When sewing, place the fabric in the sewing machine with the ruffle on top. Remove pins.

27. Place bedspread back on the bed right side up. Make sure the ruffles that are already attached are on the top of the bed rather than hanging down.

RUFFLE OVERLAP

Make sure the ruffle curves on the corner
The side ruffle should overlap the footer ruffle a few inches

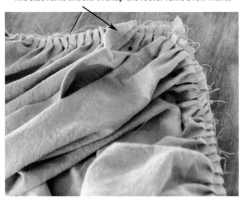

28. Now that you've attached the footboard ruffle (Ruffle 1) and the side ruffle (Ruffle 2), it's time to attach the other side ruffle (Ruffle 3). Take your black thread, and measure about 90 inches of thread. Cut it, then tie a sturdy knot in the end. Thread your needle. Do a running stitch along the top edge (not the hemmed end) about ½ inch from the top of bed Ruffle 3. Each stitch should be about ½ inch. When you are finished stitching, tie a knot at the end of the thread. This last ruffle should have a hem on each short side and the bottom side as seen in the Bed Ruffle diagram on page 123.

29. Once you have done the running stitch, place the last ruffle (Ruffle 3) on top of the bed on the left side as shown in the diagram Placement of Third Ruffle. Place the unfinished edge of the ruffle on top of the unfinished edge of piece A. The ruffle should be lying on top of your bed, right side down, not hanging off the side of your bed.

30. Spread out the ruffle, making the gathers as even as possible. Pin it in place, making sure to curve around the corner of the foot of the bed as shown. This ruffle should overlap the attached ruffle by about 3 inches on the corner. See Ruffle Overlap image on page 124. The overlap should be at least 1 inch, and no more than 3 inches.

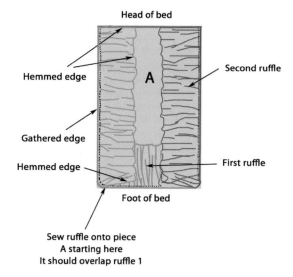

PLACEMENT OF THIRD RUFFLE

Head of bed

Hemmed edge

Second ruffle

A

Gathered edge

Hemmed edge

First ruffle

Foot of bed

Sew ruffle onto piece
A starting here
It should overlap ruffle 1

31. Sew the ruffle on, starting at the foot of the bed as shown. Sew directly on top of the running stitch with a ½ inch seam. When sewing, place the fabric in the sewing machine with the ruffle on top. Remove pins.

32. Check the bedspread to ensure you have removed all pins. Remove the black basting thread. Trim all loose threads. You have completed the bedspread! Skip down to the instructions for Making the Pillow Shams beginning with step #55.

Ruffling with a Ruffler

33. A ruffler is an attachment for your sewing machine specifically used to make a ruffle. You should be able to find a ruffler that works with your machine. If you don't have one, check with your local sewing center or try Amazon. Be sure the ruffler you select is compatible with your machine. Once you get the ruffler, you may need directions for using it. I am going to go over some basic information, but can only do so much in a book format. Please read the instructions for your specific ruffler and watch some YouTube videos on using a ruffler. Most rufflers are very similar.

34. I will attempt to offer some tips for setting up your ruffler here. Let's inspect it first because you might need to make some adjustments to it before you use it. Read through

RUFFLER DIAGRAM 1

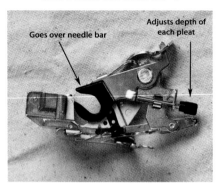

RUFFLER DIAGRAM 2

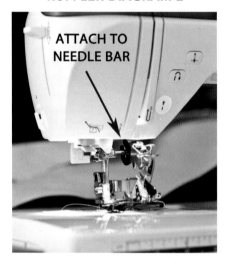

RUFFLER DIAGRAM 3

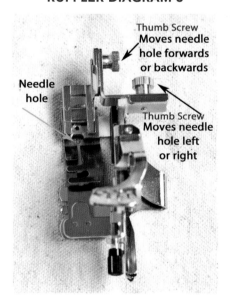

these instructions and get familiar with it before you attach it to your machine.

35. Remove the presser foot that is on your machine and attach the ruffler according to the instructions for your ruffler.

36. Be sure the black hook goes over the needle bar. See Ruffler Diagrams 1 and 2. The needle bar going up and down is what powers your ruffler attachment and makes it work. The screw shown on Ruffler Diagram 1 adjusts the depth of each pleat. Yes, it's called a ruffler, but it's actually making many, many small pleats. If you want a fuller gathering, then turn the screw clockwise. If you want a less full gather, then turn the screw counterclockwise.

37. Note the needle hole (see Ruffler Diagram 3). It is very important that you know where this is. It must line up with your needle or your ruffler won't work properly and it could possibly break your needle.

38. There are several adjustments that need to be made so that the needle lines up with the needle hole. Once you attach the ruffler to your machine, move the needle down until it almost touches the ruffler. Will the needle go through the needle hole? If not, use the thumb screws (see Ruffler Diagram 3) to adjust the horizontal and vertical alignment of the needle hole. Your ruffler might vary slightly.

The ruffler can be set to do a pleat for every stitch, every 6 stitches, every 12 stitches, or no stitches (designated with the star). See Ruffler Diagram 4. I've found that the pleat every 6 stitches is the best setting. I want my ruffles to have a double fullness, and that will get you the closest to that fullness.

39. Once you have attached the ruffler to your sewing machine and you have tested it to be sure the needle is going through the needle hole, insert some test fabric. Be sure to insert as shown in Ruffler Diagram 5. You want a ½-inch seam allowance, so try to align the edge of the fabric with the edge of the ruffler as shown in Ruffler Diagram 6. Try to sew a few stitches manually or on the lowest speed setting. Is it working properly? Do a test ruffle about 12 inches long. If it is ruffling the fabric, then take out the test fabric. Confirm that you have a ½-inch seam allowance. If not, then make sure you can get it set properly before inserting your bedspread fabric. You also need to confirm that the ruffle is set to make ruffles with a double fullness. So the 12 inches

of fabric you ruffled should be about 6 inches long now. This is important because if your resulting ruffle is less than 6 inches, you may not have enough fabric for the bedspread. Ruffler Diagram 1 shows you the screw you can adjust to make your pleats smaller or larger. Please make any needed adjustments now before you make the ruffles for your bedspread. Once you are happy it is set up properly, insert your fabric. If you need more help, please check out YouTube for ruffler videos.

40. Remember that it's vitally important that when sewing a ruffle, you sew at the lowest speed possible. If you speed up the machine, it begins to gyrate a bit and the needle moves more. As it moves, it can begin to miss the needle opening. If the needle misses the opening at a high speed, it will probably break. I have broken many, many needles, so please take heed. When you sew at the slowest speed the needle is more likely to stay aligned. And at the slower speed, if it gets out of alignment and hits the ruffler, it is less likely to break. If your needle does hit the ruffler and bends, replace it immediately.

41. Now we are ready to start sewing the ruffle for our bedspread. Follow all of the instructions I've already given. Be sure you have inserted the fabric wrong side up. Insert the fabric into the ruffler as shown in Ruffler Diagram 5. Take your time to sew the entire length of the ruffle.

42. Once you have finished making the ruffle you are ready to attach it to your bedspread topper (Piece A). Be very careful handling the ruffle. The drop cloth fabric is heavy and if you are not careful, you can easily break the thread and pull out the pleats (or ruffles).

43. Place piece A flat on top of your bed, right side up. Put the hemmed end of piece A at the head of the bed. Gently take the end of the ruffle and place it along on the foot of the bed as shown in the Placement of First Ruffle diagram on page 122. The ruffle will be too long for the foot of the bed. That's okay since we will trim it in the next step. Place the ruffle right side down. Looking at the bed from the foot of the bed, start on the right and go left as shown in the diagram. The gathered end should sit on top of the foot end. Make sure the ruffle curves around the corners as shown. Pin carefully in place as shown in the photo on page 123.

RUFFLER DIAGRAM 4

Adjusts how often a pleat is made

RUFFLER DIAGRAM 5

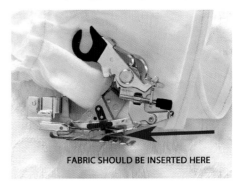

FABRIC SHOULD BE INSERTED HERE

RUFFLER DIAGRAM 6

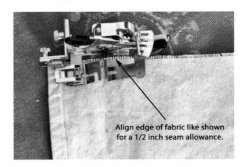

Align edge of fabric like shown for a 1/2 inch seam allowance.

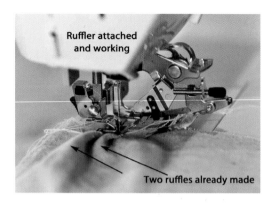

Ruffler attached and working

Two ruffles already made

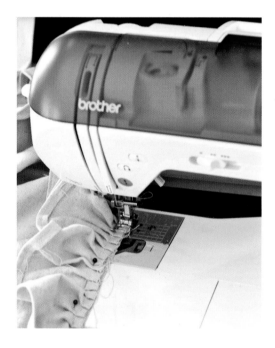

BED RUFFLE

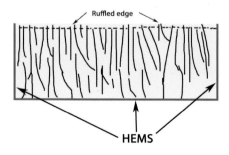

Ruffled edge

HEMS

44. At this point, the ruffle is one long piece, but we need 3 sections of ruffle for the bedspread, one for the footboard, and one for each side. We'll need to cut the ruffle into 3 sections. I don't like to do that too early, because you want the cuts to be in the correct location. As you are pinning the ruffle onto the foot of the bedspread, when you have about 1 foot left to pin, measure how much more of the ruffle you will need for the footboard ruffle and add one inch. Cut the ruffle at that point. For the section of ruffle you have pinned to piece A, you now have a raw end (where you just cut it) that needs to be hemmed. With an iron, press that end over ½ inch, then fold it over one more time and press again. Pin the hem in place. Remove the ruffler attachment from your machine and place your normal presser foot back on. Sew the hem in place. Remove pins.

45. Now finish pinning the ruffle in place. When sewing the ruffle onto the foot of the bed, start at the corner shown in Placement of First Ruffle diagram on page 122. When sewing, make sure the ruffle is on top of piece A, not underneath it. When you are sewing, sew directly on top of the basting stitch used to ruffle the ruffle.

46. Sew ruffle onto foot of piece A with a ½-inch seam allowance. Remove pins.

47. Now you should have the ruffle attached to the footboard end of piece A. We will repeat the process for each side.

48. The ruffle that is not attached to the bedspread yet needs to be cut in half. Each half will be a side ruffle. Measure the mid-point (around 80 inches or so) and cut the ruffle in two. It's okay if each ruffle is longer than that. Each ruffle should have a hem along one long end. We need to be sure that each short end also is hemmed as shown in the Bed Ruffle diagram on the left.

49. For each end of the ruffle that does not have a hem, with an iron, press that end over ½ inch, then fold it over one more time and press again. Pin and sew this hem in place. Remove pins. Check both pieces of ruffle. Are both short ends hemmed? If not, repeat this step.

50. Place bedspread back on the bed right side up. Make sure the ruffle for the foot of the bed is already attached is on top of the bed rather than hanging down as seen in the diagram, Placement of Second Ruffle on page 124.

51. Take one of the unattached ruffles and place it on the bed (right side down) as shown in the diagram Place of Second Ruffle. Pin it in place, making sure to curve around the corner of the foot of the bed as shown in the diagram. This second ruffle should overlap the attached footboard ruffle by about 3 inches on the corner as seen in the photo. The overlap should be at least 1 inch and no more than 3 inches. If as you pin the ruffle on piece A, you find there is some ruffle left over at the head of the bed, then trim the excess, press, and hem as you did before. If you find that the ruffle isn't long enough to make it all the way to the head of the bed, please see the hint in the purple box below.

52. Sew the ruffle onto piece A directly on top of the basting stitch used to ruffle the ruffle. Remove pins. You should now have the ruffle attached to the foot of your bedspread and one side.

53. Place the last ruffle on top of piece A, right side down, as shown in the diagram Placement of Third Ruffle on page 125. Pin in place. Start at the foot of the bed; be sure to overlap the ruffle by 3 inches with the ruffle at the foot of the bed. The overlap should be at least 1 inch, and no more than 3 inches. If as you pin the ruffle on piece A, you find there is some ruffle left over when you get to the head of the bed, then trim the excess, press and hem as you did before. If you find that the ruffle isn't long enough to make it all the way to the head of the bed, please

RUFFLE OVERLAP

Make sure the ruffle curves on the corner
The side ruffle should overlap the footer ruffle a few inches

SEWING RUFFLE ONTO PIECE A

see the hint in the purple box. Sew ruffle in place stitching directly over the basting seam (where you ruffled the ruffle) with a ½-inch seam allowance. Remove pins. This completes the work on the bedspread. Press and place on bed.

54. Double-check to be sure you removed all pins and press bedspread.

> Hint: Hopefully you have enough fabric. If you tested the ruffler settings before making the ruffle, it should work. But if you are short, there are a few things you can do. If it is short by just an inch or two, that is easily fixable. You can do less of an overlap at the corner. Or find a few inches of the ruffle at each end and rip out some of the ruffle. This will give you a bit of grace if you need it.

Making the pillow shams

55. I love the look of this bedspread with matching euro pillow shams. If you prefer, you can skip this step and simply use white purchased pillow shams and pillow cases. All measurements are based on a 26-inch Euro pillow insert. This pillow has an envelope closure. Yes, a zipper would be fancier, but it's also a lot more work.

56. Use the diagrams for Drop Cloths 1 and 2 to see where you should cut the pieces for the pillow shams. You will be cutting pieces, C1, C2, D1, D2, E1, E2, F1, F2, F3, and F4. Use a pencil and a yardstick to measure and mark where you should cut. Trim off the center seam that is on the drop cloth fabric. You don't need that and it will be in the way.

57. First, we will hem the two back pieces. Take D1 and press ½-inch seam along the long edge. Fold it over and press again. Pin it in place and then sew the hem. Remove pins. Take E1 and press ½-inch seam along the long edge. Fold it over and press again. Pin it in place and then sew the hem. Remove pins.

58. Next we'll make the ruffle for our first pillow. Sew the short end of F1 and F2 together. You should have a piece that is about 18 feet long.

59. Along the long end, press a ¼ fold. Fold ¼ inch again and press. Pin in place, then sew the hem.

60. Now use the technique you used on the bedspread to make a ruffle out of piece "F." For the pillow. It should be about 100 inches long once it is ruffled.

61. Take the ruffle and pin it to C1, with right sides together as in C1 with Ruffle Attached diagram. The ruffle should overlap a few inches. Be sure to round the corners like we did with the bedspread. Where the ruffle overlaps will be the bottom of the pillow (see Overlap Ruffle image).

C1 WITH RUFFLE ATTACHED

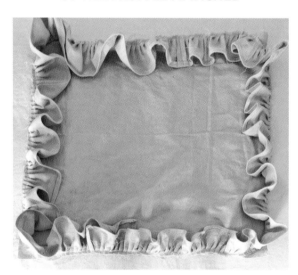

OVERLAP RUFFLE

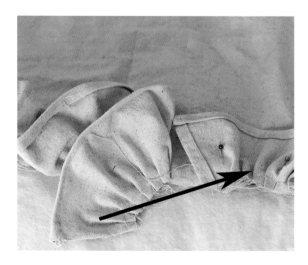

62. Baste the ruffle onto the front of the pillow sham (C1). Remove pins.

PIN D1 TO C1

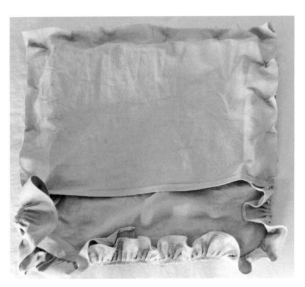

63. Place D1 on the top of C1, right sides together as shown. Pin from the C1 side. Then, place E1 on C1 as shown, right sides together. Pin from the C1 side. See pin E1 to C1.

64. Sew the pillow with a ½-inch seam allowance, being careful to follow the basting stitch you used to attach the ruffle to C1. (Be sure the side with the pins (C1) is on the top.) Remove pins as you go.

65. After sewing, make sure you have removed all pins and then trim the corners. See image Trim Corners. Turn pillow right side out.

PIN E1 TO C1

TRIM CORNERS

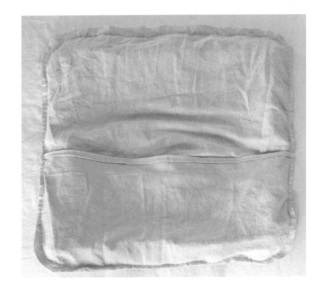

66. Repeat process for second pillow sham.

67. You've completed the bedspread. You might need to press the bedspread and pillow shams before use. Don't worry about getting rid of all the wrinkles. It's normal to have some, and that's part of the charm of natural fibers. When you remove it from your bed, gently fold it to minimize wrinkles.

CHAPTER 10: SLIPCOVERING A DINING ROOM CHAIR

It starts with an innocent enough thought, "I think this would look nice slipcovered." From there, depending on the size of the project, I either go into "this is a piece of cake" mode or the dreaded "Why, why, why? What was I thinking? This is sheer madness!" mode. I actually like sewing, but big sewing jobs can feel overwhelming, even to someone like me who has made many, many slipcovers. So my first recommendation is to start small. If you have never made a slipcover, don't start with a sofa or a wingback chair. They might cause you to break out into a cold sweat in the middle of the night. Let's say you have embraced your inner seamstress, and you have made the commitment to make a slipcover. Let's go through the steps to create a very simple, ruffled seat slipcover.

1. Buy a cushion.

    For this chair, I just happened to have an extra seat cushion that fit it perfectly. For dining room chairs, you should be able to find a cushion pretty close to the correct size. Don't worry about getting the prettiest one; it will be covered up any way.

2. Determine fabric needed.

    Now we need to figure out how much material will be needed for the slipcover. These small projects are pretty straightforward.

    a. Measure the width and depth of the seat. Mine is 16 inches wide by 15 inches deep. So use the depth to determine how much yardage is needed for the seat section. For mine, 15 inches deep, I add a ½-inch seam allowance all the way around the seat, meaning the depth needed is actually 16.

    b. Yardage needed for seat = 15 (depth) + ½ (seam allowance) + ½ (seam allowance) = 16 inches

    c. Next you will need fabric for the ruffle. First determine the height of your ruffle. I chose 5 inches for my drop, or height of the ruffle. Now I add a ½-inch seam allowance and 1 inch for the hem.

    d. The total ruffle height 5 (ruffle drop) +1 (hem) +½ (seam allowance) = 6.5 inches.

    e. Next, I take the tape measure around the outside edge of the entire seat, measuring the perimeter or circumference. I got 60 inches perimeter or 60 inches long. Since the fabric will be ruffled at roughly double the length, I double that number, and add a bit for good measure.

f. Ruffle length 60 (perimeter of seat) x 2 (extra amount needed to make ruffle) = 120 + 5 (extra amount just in case) = 125 inches.

g. 125 inches of fabric ought to be enough for the ruffle. So the ruffle fabric will be 125 inches long and 6.5 inches high.

h. Divide the total length (125) by the width of your fabric, which you may not have yet. Most are 54 inches wide or more.

i. Lengths of fabric needed for ruffle 125 / 54 = 2.3 widths of fabric.

j. That means we need 2.3 (round up to the next whole number) or 3 rows of a 6.5-inch ruffle.

k. Yardage needed for ruffle 3 rows x 6.5 ruffle length = 19.5 inches of fabric needed for the ruffle

l. Total yardage needed for project:

Yardage needed for seat + yardage needed for ruffle = total yardage needed

16 inches (needed for seat) + 19.5 inches (needed for ruffle) = 35.5 inches so I needed 1 yard (36 inches) for my project.

3. Mark fabric.

Place cushion on top of fabric. Make sure cushion is sitting on fabric straight, not crooked. Be mindful of any pattern. Place the back of the cushion near the edge of the fabric. Draw a line around the outline of the cushion. If your fabric has a pattern is it even more imperative that your fabric be straight from front to back.

4. Mark where you will cut.

The red line represents the outline of the cushion. That represents what the actual size the slipcover will be. Now measure ½ inch from the outline you drew (shown in red) on the fabric. It should be ½ inch bigger all around. We are adding the ½

inch for seam allowance. Our seam will be ½ inch. The black line represents where we will actually cut the fabric.

Then add a ½-inch seam allowance.

5. Cut fabric.

   Using the outside (black) lines you drew, cut fabric.

6. Fold fabric.

   Then fold the fabric in half to be sure the fabric is symmetrical. Trim the bigger side so that the pattern is symmetrical on both sides.

7. Cut fabric for ruffle.

   Measure a strip the length of fabric from selvage edge to selvage edge. For my project, I used 6.5 inches wide. Mark and cut this strip of fabric. Make sure to cut strips until you have enough for your project. For this project I needed 3 lengths of fabric so I cut three strips of 6.5-inch wide fabric.

8. Sew the pieces of ruffle together, end to end.

9. Press open the seams with an iron.

10. Then fold up one edge of the ruffle with a ½-inch fold, and press with iron.

11. Fold over the folded edge one more time with a ½-inch fold, and use iron to press in place.

12. Sew the hem.

13. Now you can use a ruffler to make the ruffle.

    I set mine on it to make a ruffle every 6 stitches. I also set the stitch for a distance ½ inch from the edge of the fabric.

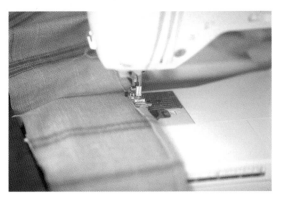

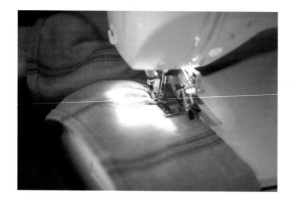

14. Now place seat fabric on the chair, right side down, then pin ruffle onto the seat fabric, with right side down. Pin along the seat fabric.

15. Leave gaps in the ruffle where chair interferes, like where the back of the chair attaches to the seat.

16. Sew ruffle onto seat, removing pins as you go.

17. Press ruffle down in place using iron.

18. Now place seat cushion on chair and place slipcover on top.

I did not add ties for the slipcover, but you could add some.

CHAPTER 11: FUN PROJECTS

Are you a "crafty" person, the kind of person who can take a toilet paper roll and make it look like an expensive napkin ring for a fancy dinner? That is not me. I am NOT crafty. However, I have a few projects that were really quite simple. I know if I can do these, so can you.

Chalkboard from a Screen Door

Talk about fun, I loved working on this chalkboard. I asked my builder Rit where I could find a screen door. He said he was getting ready to throw one out, did I want it? Yes I did! We went over to the house, and it wasn't exactly what I had in mind, but I knew it had potential. It even fit in my SUV, SCORE! After getting it home, here are the steps I went through to make the chalkboard.

1. I removed the screen and the lattice that were added by the previous owner.

2. After it was removed, I next removed the screen from the door.

3. Next I painted the red door a creamy white.

4. I found lauan at the hardware store, and I cut it to size.

5. I painted the lauan with chalkboard paint.

6. Next I attached the board to the back of the door using wood screws.

7. Cure the chalkboard paint for at least two days.

8. Take a piece of chalk and lay it flat against the board. Rub it all over the board until it is covered with chalk. This seasons the board. It took about three pieces of chalk to do the entire board.

9. Then wipe off the excess chalk using a dry cloth. Do not use a wet cloth, or you will have to start all over again.

10. Add hanging hardware on the back, and you are done. It's a simple project, but makes for a great statement piece.

Converting a Crib to a Bench

I love taking something that might otherwise be discarded and making it into something new and fun. Old iron cribs really appeal to me, but I would not want to put a real baby in one, for fear of all the safety hazards. So instead I remade this one into a bench.

1. The first thing I did was to take the front side rail off of the crib. If you can't remove that side, then you might not be able to convert the crib. The side rail on my crib came off easily.

2. The bottom did not look like it would support the weight of an adult, so I added a piece of plywood cut to the size of the crib. I made sure to cut it so that it extends past the crib framing. This way the frame supports the wood. Then I bought a brand-new mattress. They are inexpensive and readily available.

3. To make a mattress cover, I measured the length and width of the mattress, 52 inches by 27 inches.

4. I cut 2 pieces of fabric to those dimensions, adding an inch for a seam allowance in each direction. The two pieces I cut were 28 × 53.

5. Then I cut a long strip of fabric for the sides of the mattress. The width of the strip is the height of the mattress plus an inch seam allowance. The height of my mattress is 5 inches so the strip of fabric needs to be 5 inches plus 1 inch for seam allowances or 6 inches tall. The width of the fabric was 54 inches, but I needed a fabric equal to 2 × length + 2 × width. So I needed a piece with a length of 28 + 52 + 28 + 52 = 160 plus seam allowances. The fabric is 55 inches wide so I needed to cut 3 strips. Two strips means I need to add 3 inches of seam allowances so the total length of fabric I needed was 163. Three strips was just right. I cut three pieces that were 55 inches by 6 inches.

6. I sewed the three pieces end to end. Then measured the perimeter again and adjusted the last seam so that the when the pieces were all sewn into a circle where the perimeter would equal the perimeter of the mattress (160 inches).

7. I pressed those seams open.

8. I pinned the top to the side, then sewed the top to the side.

9. Then I sewed the bottom to the sides, but left one end open to insert the mattress.

10. I turned the mattress cover right side out.

11. I inserted the mattress in the opening.

12. I then finished the sewing by hand.

13. I placed the board (already cut) on the bottom of the crib.

14. Then added the mattress.

15. I could still see the board underneath the mattress as I looked at the front of the bench. A lace tablerunner tucked under the mattress covered the board and added a soft touch.

If you know how to sew and use a saw, this project is pretty basic.

This project is pretty basic if you know how to sew and use a saw.

CHAPTER 12: CARING FOR VINTAGE ITEMS

Vintage Linen

I buy a lot of vintage linens, and it's important to know how to care for them. I got these cleaning tips from my friend Martha who has been selling vintage linens for years. I have used this technique on many linen pieces and have been thrilled with the results. If your piece is an heirloom, please use a professional restoration service. Although I've used these products successfully, I cannot guarantee results. Use at your own risk.

Some old linens haven't been washed in decades and have layers and layers of dirt on them. Grain sacks are notoriously dirty. The first step is to spray any stains with OxiClean. Next soak the items in very warm water with one part powdered Tide soap, one part powdered Biz, and one part powdered OxiClean. I use about a half cup each in my tub with the water up about five inches. After 48 hours, I rinse the item and see how clean it is. The water is typically pretty dirty as you drain the water. If all of the stains are gone, then I rinse it well and I am done. If it is still stained, I repeat the process for another 48 hours. After 48 hours, I check it again. If the

stains are still there, repeat again. Martha told me she does this for up to two weeks. She says the stains are almost always gone when she is done. But if the aren't she suggests allowing the item to sit out in the sun for several days. This often allows the stain to fade.

This will not work on rust stains, but for many stains it will work.

If you are storing your linens I would make sure that the linen is completely dry. You do not want any mildew to develop. Storing damp linens especially in a plastic tub is a recipe for disaster.

I had a vintage linen tablecloth on my table and set a potted orchid on top of it. The pot was not water tight, so it leaked onto my tablecloth over the course of several months. By the time I noticed, I found a black stain under the orchid pot. It was about five inches in diameter. I would have thrown it out, except I remembered my friend Martha's advice. I used this technique and it worked.

If you are using old linen or grain sacks for sewing projects, I highly recommend that you use this technique to clean them before you do any sewing. Grain sacks will lighten in color a lot after washing.

I would avoid using bleach on vintage linen as it can weaken the fibers. It's best to let them dry while laying flat if at all possible. For rust stains, try a product called Wink that is a rust remover. Follow the instructions on the bottle.

Vintage Silver

I've read so many techniques for cleaning tarnished silver including the baking soda and water in the foiled lined pan technique, and even using catsup. I'm not sure the catsup worked any better than simply rubbing with a dry cloth. Everything I've read about chemical dips is negative, so I would avoid using that technique. Experts recommend using plain old silver polishing cream. That is what I use, and I believe that to be the best solution for cleaning tarnished silver. Silver tarnishes due to the exposure to hygrogen sulfide. Keeping it covered and away from the air can hinder the tarnishing process. I like to keep silver that I do not have displayed in treated flannel bags. The bags help protect the silver from hydrogen sulfide. Those pieces don't tarnish nearly as quickly as the pieces I have displayed. Still, I believe that if you have silver you might as well display it. I clean my silver typically twice a year. Yes, it gets tarnished in between, but I don't mind the tarnished look.

I heard once that silver can be cleaned in the dishwasher, if you don't mix it with stainless steel. I did an experiment and washed a few pieces of silverplate in the dishwasher for about a month. I used some mix-matched pieces that weren't in great shape. What happened is that the silver began to turn white. This is not unusual for silver washed in the dishwasher. I would definitely recommend that you NOT wash yours in the dishwasher.

Now for those of you that feel silverware is too high maintenance, keep in mind that if you use your silver and therefore wash it often, you will not need to polish it. The cleaning process will remove any tarnish with each cleaning.

Here are some tips for silver care:

1. Place a towel under your silverware when you are working on it.

2. Keep your silver polish jar tightly closed when not in use. You don't want it to dry out.

3. Use a Q-tip to reach inset areas or difficult to reach spots.

4. Avoid washing silver in the dishwasher.

5. Avoid exposure to salt which can corrode silver.

6. Store in flannel bags treated for use with silverware.

7. Store your silver in a dry environment.

CHAPTER 13: TABLESCAPES

I think I love hosting parties not just because I love people, but because I love food and dishes, and flowers, and silver, and pretty glasses and . . . well . . . you get the point. A pretty table just makes any party more exciting and fun. Sadly it is becoming more and more unusual to see parties where the hosts use real dishes. As a dish addict/fanatic/collector/connoisseur, I adore using my real dishes during parties. We recently had a party at our farm, where we set up tables end to end in the pasture. Most people would have used paper plates, and I tried, I really tried to use paper plates, but I couldn't do it. It had to look pretty. Paper plates are not pretty; they are practical. I had always dreamed of having a long table in a field of wildflowers—a long table covered with a white tablecloth, with wildflower vases along the length of the table. A long table covered with a white tablecloth, with wildflowers in vases along the length of the table. I pictured friends sitting at the table, enjoying a meal, savoring the company and hearty fare, children flying kites, teenagers taking off to explore the woods, and adults laughing. This was the scene for a party we held at the farm. The fields were a sea of blue as far as the eye could see. It was the kind of day that you don't want to end. We sat at the table, lingering, not wanting to leave, knowing that when someone stood the spell would be broken.

Napkins

Sometimes I use bandanas as napkins. Bandanas make for nice, large cloth napkins that are great for messy foods. I also use tea towels for napkins. They, too, are big and great for a picnic with messy foods. I also use vintage linen napkins for dinners, and I have lots of cotton napkins for less formal affairs. I love using fabric napkins for special parties or dinners. They just make it feel so special. Yes, the napkins will need to be washed and probably ironed, but if you have a party once a year, that isn't a lot of time in the grand scheme of things. It is worth it!

Set out all of your napkins so you can decide which ones go best with the dishes and tablecloth you have selected for the meal. If you have just one set of white napkins, then perfect—you are done with this step! If you have some different options, try setting several choices out on the table and decide which ones look best.

Dishes

I really, really don't like using paper plates. I try to avoid paper plates unless it is a very, very casual picnic. I know not everyone agrees with me, but I feel very strongly about using dishes when guests come over for a meal. I don't think they have to be fancy dishes, but they shouldn't be paper. I have a set of glass plates when we have a big crowd at the farm, and I prefer that to paper. When guests see you have taken the extra time to make the event special, they will adore you for creating such a magical event. It will feel like a very special party, and they will feel like they are important guests.

If variety is the spice of life, then my dishes are mighty spicy. I've got lots and lots to choose from. I love using a different set each day. When I host a tea, often each person gets a teacup with a different pattern. Some people have accused me of having two houses just so I will have more room to store all of my dishes. That is entirely not true, although I do have a china cabinet on my back porch. What? Is that wrong? You can use dishes that all match, or you can mix and match different patterns or colors. Mix and match works if you don't have enough, or if you want a more eclectic look.

If you don't have enough dishes for a party, there are a few things you can do. First, you can borrow dishes. Your neighbors or family probably have some they would be happy to loan you. The other thing you can do is buy inexpensive dishes. I bought some glass plates at Ikea for our wildflower party. They were about a dollar apiece, and so if one broke, or got lost in the pasture, I would not miss it. Another place you can usually get a good deal on dishes is a thrift or resale shop.

Flatware

I love, love, love using silverware. Sterling is so expensive, but you can still find great deals on silver-plated sets. And if you are willing to go with unmatched sets, you can get an even better deal. I also have some fun sets of flatware. There's a pink set, a black set, and bronze ware in addition to my stainless and silver-plated sets.

Tablecloth

If you don't have a lot of stuff like I do, the decision-making process will go fast. You will simply set out what you have. If you have multiple sets of dishes, you have more options, but it takes longer to decide

Bluebonnets make for a cheery centerpiece.

what to use. My first decision is where we will eat, inside out or out. Once I know what table we will be eating at, I decide which dishes we will use. After I select the dishes, next comes the tablecloth. White linen is great and goes with everything, but I also love to use vintage tablecloths. I'm looking for a tablecloth that suits my mood and goes with the dishes I want to use. Other things you can use include, burlap, a shower curtain (yes, I have used a shower curtain before), a curtain (yup on that one too), drop cloth, fabric remnant, a throw, and a towel. I use fabulous towels from Turkish T as tablecloths since they don't look like a towel at all.

Centerpiece

I use dishes and my tablecloth as a starting point. I usually look around and see if there is anything I can cut from my yard for a centerpiece: that bush that needs to be trimmed, extra flowers, or tree branches. If you don't want to spend any money on flowers, you usually don't have to. You can simply use something from your yard. If you want something specific, often you can find something pretty at the grocery store. I head over to Whole Foods or Trader Joe's for special flowers. You can go to a florist, but often you can find what you like at a nearby grocery store.

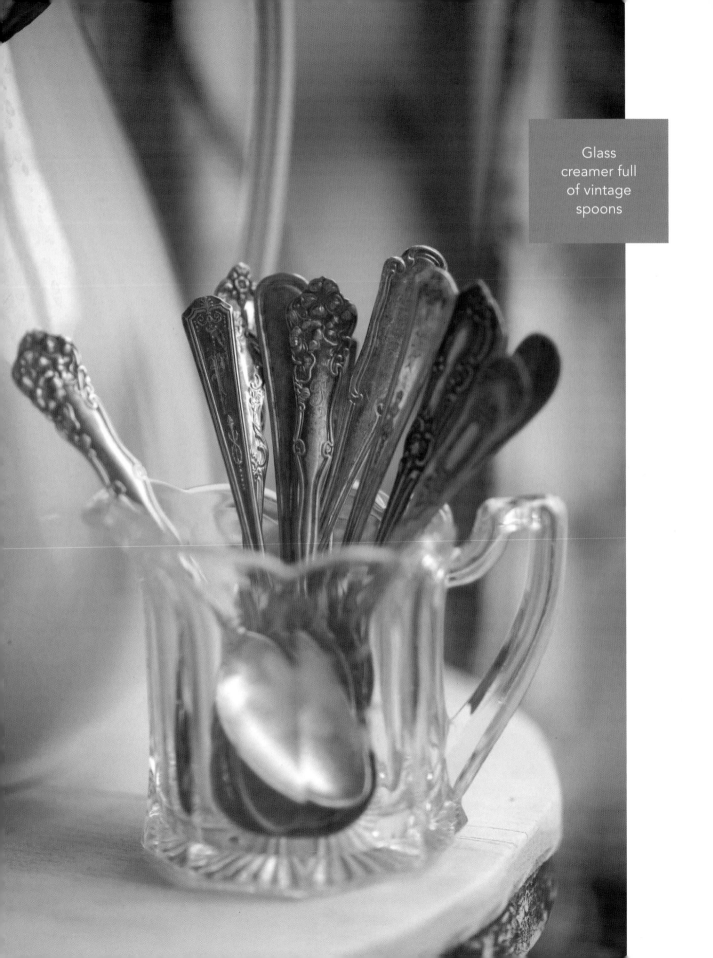

Glass creamer full of vintage spoons

If I am styling a table that won't be used for a meal, I take a different approach than if we will be using the table. If this is for a party, I avoid tall flowers or anything that might block faces and conversations across the table. Try using flowers cut so that you can see faces across the table. An individual vase on everyone's plate is nice and keeps the flowers down low. Any flowers should coordinate with your dishes and tablecloth. Look at all of the colors and see if they look good together. Colors opposite on the color wheel usually do well together.

How to Set a Table

If you are unsure about the basic table setting, you don't even need to buy an etiquette book anymore. Just use Google. The bread plate goes on the left and the drink on the right. The fork on the left and spoon and knife on the right. The napkin can go to the left of the fork or in the glass or on the plate. My mother-in-law used to do a lot of entertaining and even organized the dinners for the board of regents and board of visitors for a major hospital system in Houston, so she knew where everything went. I have to say I learned a lot from her, and that experience gave me great confidence when giving a dinner party. For dessert, the fork or spoon, whichever is being used, will be at the top of the plate. The fork will look like it was moved up there from the fork position on the right (that is how I remember the position).

So it is tines pointed to the right. The same thing goes for the dessert spoon. It is positioned as if it slid up from the right side of the plate, with the bowl of the spoon on the left. Alternately, you can provide the fork or spoon with dessert when it is served. The teacup should be closest to the spoon, followed by the wine glass, then water glass.

Drink Station

You can ask each of your guests what they want and serve it to them, or let them get their own drinks. I really, really like the "serve yourself" option. Guests can get what they want, when they want it without having to feel like they are bothering the hostess. I have found that most people prefer this option. It makes it much easier on the hostess, and frees up her time to greet guests and put those finishing touches on dinner.

Preparing the Food

It's all about having fun with your guests, so I like to have all of my food cooked and ready to go before they arrive. I do almost all of my food prep before the big day, so I am not in the kitchen the entire time my guests are here. If it is a big event, sometimes I cook for a week before and freeze items ahead of time.

With today's busy schedules, ordering from a restaurant is a great option. Just be sure to serve guests from your own beautiful dishes and not Styrofoam containers. A few weeks before the party, I put a menu together, trying to use mostly dishes that can be prepared ahead of time. If I can make it and freeze it, even better. The night before the party, if I can, I set up the table for the event, and set out the serving dishes I will be using with serving utensils.

My talented friend Therese taught us how to make these delicious raspberry macarons.

Preparation for Event

The whole point of a party is to have fun and enjoy the time with your guests. If you end up in the kitchen the entire time or if things go wrong, it might not be much fun. That is why I try to be as organized as possible to make sure it will all go smoothly. A stressed hostess makes for an awkward party. Select your menu and which dishes you will use on your table a few weeks ahead of time. Try to determine your menu and decide what you will use on your table a few weeks ahead of time. Then I do as much food prep as possible the day before or early on the day of the party. Another tip is to only cook things you have already made in the past. Don't experiment when cooking for a crowd. You don't want any nasty surprises. I write out what needs to be done and check off my list as I go.

Dealing with Disaster

If you are prepared and organized, doing as much cooking as possible in advance of your event, and using tried-and-true recipes, you will minimize the chances of a disaster. For example, don't make soufflés, which can easily fall, unless you are a very seasoned cook and know what you are doing. Minor problems have a way of happening: you may run out of ice, an appetizer might burn, or you might have forgotten to salt a dish. Try to take all of this in stride. Your guests will be very forgiving. Try not to call attention to it; just do the best you can. If you have to mention it, laugh it off. If it is bad, and you mention it, guests will feel the need to build you back up. She suggests just moving forward and fixing things as best you can. For big disasters, a different approach may be needed. If your main dish is burned or the dog eats your dessert, you will not be able to move forward and just ignore it. If the worst happens, you can always explain what happened and order pizza, or a cake at the bakery. It will make for quite the story back

at the office the next day. Just try to have fun. Life is made up of experiences, and when things go wrong, I try to learn from them, and get a laugh. Mistakes aren't the end of the world. If you have invited good friends, they will be very supportive of you if things do go wrong. Rarely, rarely have I seen such a disaster. Usually the problems are quite minor, and often go unnoticed by guests. Just have fun!

CHAPTER 14: THE KITCHEN, HEART OF THE HOME

The kitchen is one of the most important rooms in a home. This is the room where the family spends time preparing meals, and often where they share a meal as well. This is where guests tend to gather during parties, no matter how fancy the dining room is. A well-designed kitchen is not only a piece of art, but it also can be very functional. If you like to cook and bake like I do, then you probably spend a large chunk of time in the kitchen every day. Even if you don't cook much, people still use their kitchens to heat up take-out, or to eat breakfast. Since you probably spend a good deal of time in here, it's important that you enjoy this room. And the more you enjoy it, the more time you will want to spend there. Even if you don't enjoy cooking, having a beautiful kitchen just might win you over to the joy of cooking. Chores like washing dishes are so much more tolerable in a pretty kitchen, or maybe that's just me.

There isn't just one look that says "French kitchen" to me. There are so many different kitchen touches that evoke a French attitude. You don't need to rip out your current kitchen and install a brand new one to get French accents. It's amazing how adding French accents in small doses can still give a room a big impact. Work with what you have to give your kitchen a fresh, exciting look. I have included some updates that are simple and inexpensive, along with some that are more involved and expensive. The list is not meant to be a definitive one, but simply a list of ideas to help you figure out what will work in your home.

I love the feel of a traditional country French kitchen with stone walls, open shelving, a farmhouse sink with a skirt, and a big pine table. Most of us don't have a kitchen like that. But that's okay. There's plenty of things we can incorporate into our kitchens to create a little French *je ne sais quoi.*

Decorating with Dishes

I adore dishes, and have been collecting them since I was in college. I knew I had too many, but then my collection doubled when my mother-in-law passed away, leaving all of her dishes to me. She, too, was a collector of dishes. Now I was in a predicament. What was I going to do with over ten sets of dishes, along with many odd pieces? And on her death bed (I am not making this up), she begged me to keep all of her good stuff. I patted her hand, smiled, and told her I would do the best I could. Then after I left the room, I groaned. Seriously, four people only need so many dishes, and I was already way over my limit. I kept as many as I could absorb, then sold and gave away what was left.

I was still overrun with dishes, and so I have gotten very creative over the years on how I display my dishes. There are lots of ways to display dishes, and they are easy to incorporate into most any room. I draw the line at the bathroom. Oh, I spoke too soon. I do keep a little teacup full of lavender in there.

Open shelving is perfect for storing dishes. To give a collection a cohesive look, I suggest you use dishes of just one color. White dishes are fabulous, and they look wonderful when displayed.

You can also display dishes in a wire shelf. I love this one with the white ironstone. Notice that again, all of the dishes are white. Collecting things of all one color gives the collection a unifying theme.

And I don't like to limit the display of dishes to the kitchen.

I love to display them anywhere I can. I found a little cabinet at auction that I use to display dishes. It wasn't until after I brought it home that I realized what it was—the top of any old grandfather clock case. Someone before me removed the clock itself and added a shelf. Now it is a funky way to show off extra teacups and other goodies.

Kitchen Updates

I'm all about working with what you have, so I would never suggest your rip out your kitchen, unless that is what YOU want! So, what can you do to make it feel more French? Here are a few ideas. I've broken them down into expensive updates and budget-conscious updates. Some of the ideas are more elegant, and some rustic.

Expensive Updates

1. *Paint cabinets white.* It may be considered a trend, but I do think it is a good solution for updating a kitchen. Some stained cabinets end up looking dated. The white cabinets have more of a timeless look. Although I love the look of stained cabinets, they often look outdated faster than white cabinets.

2. *Change out counter tops and backsplash if needed.* Subway tile is a great way to go. My suggestion is to go simple and neutral. You probably won't be in this house forever, and a trendy tile could seriously date your kitchen and reduce its value.

3. *New countertops, if needed.* Marble is stunning and gorgeous, but not very practical for people who actually use their kitchen. If you want a similar look, that doesn't etch or stain as easily, you can try white granite, quartz, or quartzite. If you do insist on marble, try the honed version. If the marble becomes etched, it won't be as obvious.

4. *Reface cabinets.* This option doesn't require the cabinets to be replaced, but they will look brand new.

5. *Add beams.* They seem to have universal appeal. Here is what I noticed in my home: When we have visitors, most of them comment about how much they like the beams. The strange thing is how the beams have such a chameleon effect. People that like

Another way to display dishes is in a plate rack.

You can go with all white or a mix of pattterns.

English style tell me they look so "Tudor." Someone from Alaska, said the beams reminded him of home, and my fellow Francophiles think they look French. That may explain why everyone likes them. They say "cozy and warm" no matter what your preferred style is.

But for those of us that love French style, the exposed beams really make a home feel French. We found our reclaimed beams at a salvage yard nearby. They still have bits of paint on them here and there. If you love the look, and are lamenting the lack of beams in your house, did you know they can usually be added later for probably less than you think? Except for the big beam down the middle of our kitchen, the rest are not load bearing and were added like crown molding. If you have crown molding now, that will probably need to be removed.

6. *Update appliances.* Stainless is usually the safest bet for the look and resale, although there are some charming vintage-looking appliances in various colors available on the internet. If you really want a French look (and have a generous budget), you can always add a French stove like La Cornue or Lacanche.

7. *Change out your vent hood.* You can go with something rustic and fun, like an old awning, or something more traditional.

8. *Update bar or counter stools.* Gorgeous Louis XVI counter stools (see page 174) may seem too fancy for a kitchen, but why not? The fabric is actually an easy-care synthetic that resists stains. So you can have something very French and lovely that is also comfortable and practical.

9. *Update doorknobs.* For door knobs, I chose crystal knobs with a curvy plate. I love the idea of using antique door knobs, but if you do, keep in mind you probably won't be able to find a full matching set for your home. If you want to use antique door knobs, you will probably need to use door knobs that are mismatched, since I can never find more

than two or three that match. I used new knobs, and they all look the same.

10. *Add built-in and open shelving to display dishes, crystal, silver, and really whatever you have.*

11. *Add a plate rack.* I asked my carpenter to add big plate racks on either side of my breakfast room window, but you can add a much smaller plate rack and still get a big impact.

12. *Convert some of your cabinet doors to glass front doors.* I love the look of the glass doors. It is a great way to show off your dishes without exposing them to dust.

Budget-Conscious Updates

1. *Clean off your countertops, so that you have fewer things sitting out.* It's a no-cost solution that really makes your kitchen look better.

2. *Update lighting and add a chandelier where you can.* You will probably need to hire a licensed electrician for this electrician work. Light fixtures can look dated after a while. When you change them out, look for something that you love!

3. *Add removable shelving.* This can be done using boards and brackets to display dishes, or by adding a pre-made shelving unit. This type of shelving is not permanent and can be removed when you move. Another plus is that it can often be added by the homeowner.

4. *Use baskets for storage.* Here the homeowner used a large basket to hold cookie sheets and other kitchen supplies.

5. *Use vintage scales.* I suppose you could use them to actually weigh ingredients, but I like to use them for décor purposes only.

6. *Add some ironstone.* I love to use ironstone in décor. Setting out an ironstone pitcher or platter adds a special touch in just about any kitchen.

7. *Add a bottle-drying rack.* These drying racks were originally made to dry wine bottles, but they are so charming when used to display mugs, cups, or glasses.

8. *Use pretty vintage containers to hold silverware.* This pressed glass vases holds silver spoons near the coffee maker in a guesthouse. The guests staying here are bound to feel special.

9. *Use something unexpected as your spoon rest.* I use a pretty plate or pressed glass bowl. I have yet to see a spoon rest that I like. So why not find something pretty in your cupboard and make it work as a spoon rest?

10. *Add some fun vintage accessories like rolling pins, old utensils, and collectibles like a vintage lemon press.*

11. *Add enamelware.* The enamelware pitchers from France have a very unique look with an inverted cone shape, while their American cousins have more of an hourglass shape. I personally like both.

12. *Update the cabinet pulls.* Cabinet pulls are very easy to replace. Usually the process takes minutes per pull or knob, and requires just a screwdriver. The cost per pull or knob varies greatly, but those on a budget can usually find something nice for a reasonable price.

13. *Use old pitchers to hold your spoons and whisks.* It's okay if it gets a bit tarnished. It's called "patina." I leave any plastic spatulas in the drawer, and just put the stainless and wood utensils in my pitcher for aesthetic reasons.

> This pressed glass vase holds silver spoons near the coffeemaker in a guesthouse.
>
> The guests staying here are bound to feel special.

14. *Store ripening fruit in pretty bowls or containers.* It seems we often have fruit sitting about in our kitchen as we wait for it to ripen. So my philosophy is why not display that fruit in a pretty bowl? When you skip the plastic bowl, and use a bowl from your collection, it goes from practical storage to a work of art.

15. *Add a piece of furniture to your kitchen.* If your kitchen is small, you probably won't be able to add any furniture in there, but if you can, it gives your kitchen a warm, cozy feel, like an old kitchen before the days of lots and lots of cabinets.

16. *Display only dishes of one color in your kitchen.* I had dishes of all colors in my cabinets, because I collect dishes. But then I moved all of those dishes out and just put in white dishes. And guess what happened? I loved it! It looks better because all of the dishes now look like they belong to the same collection.

The walls are covered in shiplap, the island is topped with wood, and the counters are marble.

It's amazing how much character the owner added in such a tiny space.

Round Top Rustic Kitchen

This rustic kitchen is full of charm. The homeowner nailed her Texas farmhouse French look. Tucked away down a sleepy dirt road, this abode works as a charming weekend getaway home. What it lacks for in size, it more than makes up for in style. This homeowner took the time to incorporate lots of reclaimed materials. The beams, walls, cabinetry, flooring, shelving, and even the island are all made from reclaimed materials.

The cabinetry has been sealed, so there is no need to worry about the paint peeling. The island is my very favorite part of this kitchen. It's gorgeous in its simplicity. You rarely see a pot filler over the stove in such a compact kitchen, so this one is a rare luxury.

Guest Cottage

This is yet another small kitchen packed with charm. This guest cottage is also full of reclaimed materials, and is oozing with warmth and fun. It's very casual, and beckons guests to come in and make themselves at home.

Dishes openly displayed like these vintage white ironstone pieces provide character. Using open shelving like this wire shelf is a great way to add storage to a small kitchen.

Elegant Farm Kitchen

The wood trough on the island and the basket pendant light provide warm farmhouse details to the upscale city kitchen. A long antique farmhouse table works well in the space, while the large gas stove provides ample room to cook. The narrow table works beautifully for the empty-nester owners.

Using antiques in the kitchen warms up the space and makes it cozy.

A pretty soup tureen gives the table color and character.

The Blue Kitchen

This charming kitchen is very warm and unique with its blue cabinets and AGA stove, an unusual sight in Texas. The beams add a French touch to this English-styled kitchen. The copper sink gives the room warmth and character.

One of the best features of this kitchen is how it opens up to this incredible courtyard.

Tiny Kitchen

This little studio apartment is perfectly sized for one person. It's currently used as guest quarters, but could be a full-time apartment. The white subway tile and quartzite countertop give the brand new kitchen a fresh, cheery feel. The refrigerator is full-sized. A vintage Italian-made Louis XV card table works beautifully in such a small space. A little cupboard is an antique French piece that holds silverware and linens.

Shabby Kitchenette

This tiny little kitchenette is in a very small space set up for guests. With just a sink, a tiny fridge, and a microwave, guests are set for an overnight stay. Silverware sits in a little crystal vase, ready for guests to make their own fresh cup of coffee.

My Kitchen

The reason we ended up building a new house, rather than buying an existing house, comes down to the kitchen, pure and simple. I wanted this exact kitchen and couldn't find a home with this look. I wanted it to be open to the living room, to have a separate breakfast room, a big island, large refrigerator, glass-front cabinets, farmhouse sink, a butler's pantry with open shelving, plate racks, and a 48-inch gas range. As the plan evolved, we added the rustic beamed ceiling, the crackled subway tile, and the white granite. The kitchen/living room is by far the biggest space in the house, and it's where we hang out as a family. I wanted something elegant yet cozy, something grand yet inviting. I knew we would have to work to make the room feel cozy with lots of white and the 10-foot ceilings. Rustic beams and tiles with a hint of color helped to warm the space. Plates in the plate rack, the big stove, and comfy stools at the counters gave the room the feeling of a warm embrace.

CHAPTER 15: DINING SPACES

Some people feel the idea of a dining room is completely outdated. I still really like the idea of a dining room, because it is a place set aside for meals with family and friends. Notice I didn't say FORMAL dining room. I don't feel it has to be formal, but I like having a nice-sized space for dining. It is great to have a place to entertain. There is nothing wrong with eating in the kitchen or breakfast room; the dining room is usually bigger so it can accommodate more people. I like to have a space that will accommodate not only my family of four, but also a few other people. Whatever the configuration in your home, it's about making it comfortable for you and your family. I strongly believe having meals together is important to a family, so it is a passion of mine to create spaces that embrace lingering at the table and conversation. If it is uncomfortable, people will be in a hurry to leave, and that does not encourage long conversations. Chairs need to be comfortable and the space needs to be inviting. I want the space to be soft but lively, beautiful but approachable, elegant but not stuffy. In short, I want it to be big on elegance and charm, while at the same time being comfortable and cozy.

Common Dining Room Mistakes

1. Table too big for space

    All too often I see tables that are too big for the dining room. If you have to hold in your breath to squeeze past the table, it's too tight. Feeling jammed into a corner is not conducive to lingering.

2. Too formal

    Beautiful is one thing, formal and stiff is another. Make sure your dining room is inviting. If your room seems too formal, try adding some warm, casual touches to the room to tone it down, like baskets, crates, rustic fabrics, or woods. Vintage items also can help make the space feel cozy. You want your guests to relax, not feel like if they touch something it will break.

3. Window coverings dated

    Window treatments can sometimes be dated looking in the dining room, which does not invite lingering. For dining rooms with dated window coverings, you can simply remove them and leave the windows bare. Or you can hang some simple premade sheers for a soft look.

4. Too matchy-matchy

    I prefer to have an assortment of pieces that look like they were collected over time. Usually my chairs don't match the table. So if you have a table, chairs, and a china cabinet that all match, you might want to consider changing something out. The newer look is actually to avoid a china cabinet all together.

Breakfast Room

A mix of the rustic with the refined is a look I lean toward in décor. This corner of our home houses a lovely French antique armoire that I had converted to a china cabinet. The silvering on the mirror was removed, so that it is now clear, and we added shelves. It is juxtaposed against the rustic antique beams and the casual French lantern. I paired the antique French table with casual, vintage caned chairs.

The built-in plate racks also add interest to this breakfast room. Plates can be changed out with the seasons, or the look can be changed out by changing the plates. It also provides much-needed storage for large platters. I find that they can look boring when I just use white platters, so I've added some plates with soft colors.

Round Top Farmhouse

For this open-concept Round Top farmhouse, casual is the way to go. The look is very relaxing, with a hint of elegance. A large demijohn, an ironstone pitcher, and a simple linen table runner give the room rustic appeal. The antique table is also perfectly beautiful and rustic.

The burlap host chairs are comfortable and add wonderful texture to the room.

City Dining Room

Here in the dining room, I used pinks and whites with just a touch of blue in the rug. I used a cascading effect with the mirror in the back then down to the console against the back wall, the back chairs, the dining room table, down to the bench, and then to the floor. Using a bench makes the room feel much more open, since you can see the entire table. The glass bottles add height without making the room feel closed off.

Rather than using a traditional china hutch, I used a rustic console to add an unexpected twist to the dining room. Think of things that will work well together, but aren't matched. Also try to think of new and unique ways to decorate your room. The vintage French chairs don't match the table, but they work well together.

Farm Dining Area

Our farmhouse is small, about 1,000 square feet. It feels much larger because the living room, dining room, and kitchen are all one big room. To add elegance and comfort to our farm kitchen, we went with upholstered French round back chairs.

A round gateleg table is flexible because each side can be dropped. When purchasing a table, look at your space to see if it is basically square or rectangular. A round or square table might work best for a square room, while a rectangular table often works best with a longer dining room. I replaced a small square table with this round one, because the square table could only seat 4 people. The round table can seat eight people comfortably when needed, but the sides can also be let down when seating is just needed for four or less. If you have a small space but need a larger table when guests come, try a drop leaf table or a small table with leaves. The drop leaf tables usually will fit in a smaller space than a table with leaves. For this table, with leaves up, it is five feet in diameter, with both leaves down, it's about eighteen inches by five feet.

Houston Heights House (First Edition)

This dining room is in a beautiful new craftsman-style home in the Houston Heights. Notice how the room doesn't have anything that matches. It's a collected look that feels like things were acquired over time.

Notice that the homeowner selected a very modern version of a china cabinet that looks like a bookcase with doors. This type of china cabinet can really update a dining room space. It gives it a fresh look while still providing storage for china and silver.

The mirror in this room has a gorgeous patina.

Mirrors are nice for dining rooms to reflect the light.

The finish on this mirror is exquisite.

English Cottage

This home is new, but it was built in a very traditional English cottage style. The beams look very much in keeping with the English feel of the home, and yet they are quintessentially French at the same time. The banquette makes use of a small space and allows for flexible seating.

Soup tureens are great pieces to display since they have are more three-dimensional than a plate. Everybody seems to love them.

Vintage or new, they add so much warmth to a room.

China Cabinet Alternatives (First Edition)

If you take a close look at these rooms, not one of them contains a traditional china cabinet. One has a cabinet in the dining room, but it is more of a cupboard than a traditional china cabinet. If you want to give your dining room that designer look, I suggest something you may find radical. Either get rid of your china cabinet, or paint it. Now this idea may be too "out there" for some, and if it doesn't appeal to you, then keep your china cabinet as is. Don't ever feel the need to implement someone else's ideas if you don't like them. This is something to consider if you want to do something totally different. You do not have to have a china cabinet in your dining room. It is not required by law, although some of us were raised to believe that. I don't have a china cabinet in my dining room. If you choose not to have a china cabinet, there are many other options.

If you go with something shorter than a china cabinet, like a console (mine is about thirty inches tall), be sure to add a mirror or artwork above the console to add interest to the room. If you are unsure about getting rid of your china cabinet, try emptying it and moving it out of the dining room for a week to see if you like the look. If you are missing your china cabinet, it is still there, and you can put it back. If, however, you decide you like the new openness of the dining room, you can now get rid of it with more confidence. I like to call this

WHAT YOU CAN USE INSTEAD OF A CHINA CABINET

1. Open shelving

2. Wall shelf

3. Armoire

4. Console

5. Buffet

reversibility. Before I get rid of a piece, I move it out of the room to be sure I like the room without it. If I am undecided, I keep the old piece around for a week while I think about. Usually, I know right away if I want to keep or get rid of something. Some people need more time to decide, and for them, a temporary move is best.

CHAPTER 16: THE LIVABLE LIVING ROOM

The living room, family room, den, or keeping room, is the room where you spend time with family and friends. This is where the family unwinds after a long day, where you entertain family and friends. Although I love an elegant look, the living room also needs to be practical and VERY comfortable. I want comfy places to sit and visit, a cozy spot to curl up with a good book and a cup of tea. I want a seating arrangement that encourages talking. It is a modern age in which we live, so most living rooms have a television. I know that needs to be factored in as well, but I don't want the TV to become what the room is about. The living room needs to be inviting. The sofa and chairs need to say "come curl up and read a book," or "let's have a conversation."

I am a homebody. I sometimes hate to admit it, but it's true. I think that is why I enjoy feathering my nest so much. Home is where I want to be; it nourishes my soul. It welcomes friends and embraces my family. The living room is where much of that interaction happens.

Comfortable and Elegant

The living or family room is where the family spends time together, where they entertain friends, and where they live. Not to put too fine a point on it, but this is an important room. I like to accomplish two things with this room.

1. Give the room presence and elegance.

2. Make the room warm, welcoming, and comfortable.

I think a lot of people feel the need to decide whether the room will be comfortable or elegant. Why not both? It can be done! Sure, some beautiful chairs are not comfortable, but there are many comfortable chairs that are also elegant. I like to add a pretty, delicate chair in the room for form, but then make sure there is plenty of comfortable seating for people to actually use. The pretty chair I like to add to a room is probably not the most comfortable chair in the room, so it probably won't get much use, but it still needs to be sturdy enough for someone to actually sit in it. If you add a chair to a public room in your house, someone will sit in it whether you want him to or not. If you do have a chair that isn't sturdy enough for seating, I recommend you put it in your bedroom where you are more certain someone won't actually use it. If, however, you do even up with a delicate chair in the living room, I highly suggest putting a stack of books or something else in the chair to discourage use.

Selecting Furniture

I like to start with a full-sized comfy sofa. I feel strongly that every living room should have a sofa, unless one won't fit in the room. It needs to be big enough for taking a nap (that is our rule at least). Everyone in our family likes to take a nap, and there's always a race to see who gets to the sofa first at our house on Sunday afternoons. It's first come, first serve.

I don't worry about the sofa being French. It needs to be comfortable, since it will probably be one of the most used pieces of furniture. Pick a silhouette that you like. There are so many choices: exposed legs or skirted sofas, high backs or low backs, big arms or low arms, three cushions or two.

I recommend a three-cushion sofa or a one-cushion sofa. If you get a two-cushion sofa, it turns into seating for just two.

A taller back sofa works well in a room with very tall ceilings.

A shorter back sofa works well in a room with lower ceilings.

Make sure your sofa will fit through your front door. (I learned that one the hard way.)

I really like sofas with slipcovers, so you can clean the slipcover if need be. A slipcover isn't necessary, but it's a nice bonus if available. This way you have two looks, with the slipcover and without. The slipcover should be washable, since the point is that it can be removed and washed. Sometimes you can buy new sofas with a slipcover. That would be ideal since buying a custom-made slipcover is very expensive.

I make my own slipcovers, and I ADORE a slipcovered sofa, but I would not enjoy paying for a custom-made slipcover. The slipcovers are washable, they extend the life of the sofa, and they can give a sofa with good bones a totally new look. My sofa is a strong red color. I'll bet you didn't know that. Rather than throw it out when I changed to a neutral palette, I made custom slipcovers. It was much less expensive than buying a new sofa, but slipcovering requires advanced sewing skills. Since I used Italian linen, the fabric was not cheap. Having a custom slipcover made is close to the cost of replacing your sofa.

As for fabric, I prefer a solid color. Patterns come and go. Nothing will date your sofa faster than a

strong pattern. Having worked in a furniture store, this is a lesson I learned early on. Avoid a patterned sofa! A sofa with a solid color is going to stay in style much longer. Think wallpaper versus paint. As much as I love wallpaper, I have to admit it looks dated in a very short time. And if you go with a pattern, then you will be much more limited as to what will go with the sofa fabric. If you are someone who loves patterns, add them with throws and pillows. Pillows are much cheaper to replace than sofas.

If you are starting from scratch, I recommend selecting your sofa first. Then let that decision drive everything else. You can almost always find paint to coordinate with your sofa, but it isn't always easy to find a sofa you like that coordinates with your paint color. I prefer neutral fabric, but that may not be for you. If you want color, then go for the color. As I said, I recommend a solid color on the sofa. If you want a particular pattern in the room, why not use it on pillows and maybe a throw? When you become bored with the pattern, and you will, then the cost of changing out the pattern is the cost of a few pillows versus the cost of a sofa. The sofa is one of your big money purchases, and you want to stay happy with it as long as possible.

I have purchased two sofas with patterns that I quickly tired of and couldn't wait to replace. The patterns were strong, bold patterns. I replaced them not because they were threadbare or worn, but because I was tired of those patterns. If you insist on a patterned sofa, try a pattern that is subtle and timeless.

After the sofa is selected, I like to add a French chair, or two, or three. The fastest way to make your room look French is to add one or more French chairs. Just keep in mind that the chairs need to be comfortable. You can always use large comfortable club chairs in the room for "real use" and just add a pretty "fru fru" French chair in the corner that just holds books, that no one actually uses.

As for the chairs in the room, there are a lot of directions you can go here. Club chairs are fine, and I would definitely consider comfort as much as looks. I used French settees in my living room instead of chairs. I think they are quite comfortable, but not as comfortable as a club chair would be. It's best to actually sit in the chairs if you can before purchase. If you are buying online, look for chairs that have lots of positive reviews

There are lots of gorgeous choices for coffee tables, but I end up most of the time using an ottoman, since my feet end up there. Comfort is a factor, and an ottoman usually looks

pretty good as a coffee table. When selecting an ottoman, look for one with pretty legs to add a layer of beauty to your room. That is a way to add style to the room without compromising on comfort.

All of the wood furniture does not need to match, but you don't want it to clash. For example, a red-based mahogany piece may not mix well with an antique pine piece. I avoid very glossy mahogany and

Slipcovered linen chairs and ottoman.

cherry woods in general. They seem more eighteenth-century English to me than French. I look for antique pine, walnut, and rustic raw woods. A few years ago, my entire house was done in mostly high-gloss mahogany. I mention it because I hear people say they are tired of mahogany but are stuck because their house is full of it. Even if you are on a tight budget, that may not be entirely true. Often, you can sell your old pieces on Craigslist and in consignment stores. With the money you make, you can buy used furniture very cheaply.

If you love the bones of a piece, but don't like the stain and finish, you can always paint it if you choose. I have painted my share of furniture, but I try to not overdo it. I don't want every piece of furniture in my home to be painted. I think balance is important. Painting is a fabulous solution; I just suggest that you don't paint everything.

I like to have a least a few pieces of French furniture in every room. It doesn't take much to give a room a French feel, just one or two pieces. I found one French table at an antique auction for $25. The top isn't in the best condition, but I think that just adds character; a perfectionist would run screaming from my house, because most of my furniture is in less than perfect condition. My furniture is well loved, and has some scratches and dents here and there. I don't worry about imperfections. If you buy vintage and antique furniture, it becomes increasingly difficult to find perfect furniture, the older it is. Once you get it home, the dog is going to bump into it, someone will kick it or drop something on it, so save yourself some grief and embrace the imperfections of furniture and those of the people in your life. In the long run, you'll be much happier.

Little tables are fairly easy to find at thrift and resale stores. I don't necessarily look for a French table, but a table with character. If you aren't excited about something . . . DON'T BUY IT. Seriously, don't. buy. it. You will never like it, and you will either end up getting rid of it later or secretly wishing you could get rid of it. It will be the piece you accidentally leave outside in the rain. Antique and vintage tables are usually easy to find, reasonably priced, and have a lot more character than new ones.

Furniture Arrangement

It is difficult to talk about how the furniture should be arranged in your room without seeing it. Still, there are a few rules of thumb I like to keep in mind. I like the room to be set up so that it looks its best from the direction in which you enter the room. Of course you also need to make sure that the television can be seen from all chairs, and the same goes for a fireplace. The furniture should be arranged around the fireplace as well. Depending on the size of the room, and the amount of furniture in the room, you may have more than one seating area. Make sure the room flows, and also consider the traffic patterns.

Here are a few of my suggestions:

1. Don't just push all of the furniture to the walls. Make sure chairs are close enough for those seated to have a conversation. If the room is large, then break it up into two or more seating areas.

2. Try to arrange things so what you see as you enter the room is the best view of the room. First impressions are important for rooms as much as they are for people. I know you've heard it before, but you only get one chance to make a good first impression. Make it count. This is the view that guests will most likely remember.

3. Try to edit out extraneous furniture. Too much furniture makes the room feel cramped and uninviting. I know it's difficult, but you'll be glad you did.

4. For bedrooms, I like the bed to be on the opposite wall of the door if possible. I want to walk in and see the headboard from the door.

5. Buy some sliders and move the furniture around to try different arrangements.

6. Another helpful thing to do is draw your room layout on grid paper and then make templates of all your furniture. Make sure your templates and the room are all to scale for the exercise to be of value. I used this idea extensively before we moved. This worked for 90% of our furniture. Only a few pieces didn't work as planned.

Working with Built-ins

I've got mixed feelings about built-in furniture. It is great to have large bookcases or other built-in features since they are wonderful for storage and require that less furniture be purchased. If they are beautiful, then they can add drama and presence to the room. If they are unattractive, then you are pretty much stuck with them, and you sometimes end up trying to make them work when they just don't.

For built-ins to be an asset to a room, they need to be well designed. I wanted my built-in features to look custom, so I worked with the carpenter to ensure they looked more like furniture. Sometimes we are stuck with built-ins designed by someone else. So what do you do if they are uninteresting? You or your carpenter can add details to the cabinetry to make it more appealing. Trim can often be added or even removed. Depending on your budget, you could also have the built-in cabinets or shelves removed. One of my clients chose to remove built-in units that were in several rooms. The bedrooms looked so much better with the cabinetry removed, and now those bedrooms can be configured many different ways. Before this change, furniture layout options were very limited. You can also alter cabinetry with paint. Look on Houzz.com and Pinterest.com to find ideas.

Styling Bookcases

There are so many thoughts on how to properly style a bookcase, and there are so many ways to do it well. Here are my thoughts. Use vintage books. I know it sounds obvious, but people don't always put books in bookcases. One time I filled mine with dishes. Did I say that out loud?

Sometimes, to give the bookcase a uniform look, I turn the books backwards so the spine faces the back of the bookcase. I like the look from a decorator's standpoint, but some people don't like this look, because you can't easily find a particular book in your bookcase. If it is a working library, then clearly this approach isn't going to work. If, however, the bookcase is filled with books that you rarely read, this look might be for you. Using the books turned backwards means they all have a uniform neutral white and creamy look. If the spines face out, then there will probably be all colors of book spines showing. That isn't as visually pleasing as just using one color palette.

Another tip I have for giving your bookcase French feel is to add vintage items. They don't even have to be French. Having vintage items in a bookcase often gives it a French feel. You can use old cameras, clocks, bookends, silver trophies, and bottles, just to name a few things.

Styling a Fireplace

How you style a fireplace is important to the design of your home because the fireplace is often the main focal point for the room. And yet I think it is one of the most difficult places to decorate because of limitations such as the mantel size and the size of the space above the mantel.

There are also heat issues, since there is potential for a roaring fire below. Many homeowners use this space for a flat-panel TV. I prefer to not put the TV there, but often there is no other place for the TV, so it has to go above the fireplace.

When the television is above the fireplace, that means there are even more limitations to how you can decorate the space. Now you have to consider if something will block the view of the TV. If you have a TV above the mantel, the best thing to do might be not putting anything on

the mantel. In my home, I had a cabinet built in the wall to house our TV. When the TV is not on, the doors are closed. Still, I can't put anything too tall on my mantel or it will get knocked over when the doors are opened. Putting something below or to the side of the television works better.

Why Go Neutral?

I love color. I mean, I *love* it. I have appreciated neutral homes for years in magazines and books, but I was one of the people that said I could never do that. I warmed to the idea

gradually. At the end of the day if you don't want to go neutral, then don't! It's YOUR house. For those of you that want to know my reasons for going neutral, here they are.

So why did I go neutral?

Neutral Is Classic

I kept seeing neutral rooms, and as it always seems to happen, the more you see a trend, the more you warm to it. I saw gorgeous room after gorgeous room done in soft colors or neutrals. Meanwhile my entire home was done in red, gold and yellow. I began to really like the look, but I refused to get rid of all my expensive upholstered furniture. How could I ever hope to switch to neutrals? Even my walls were yellow. Over time I decided I would make the switch, although I knew it would be a difficult change.

Neutral Is Flexible

I have had three or four different sets of pillows I have used on my white linen sofa. When I had a strong pattern on my sofa, I couldn't find any pillows that would work, except the ones that came with the sofa. If you can't change out the pillows on a sofa, then you really are stuck with the same look every day, every week, every month. People typically tire of a non-neutral sofa sooner than they do with a neutral one. If you like to change things often, then you may tire of your sofa sooner than you would a neutral one. A white sofa has a lot more options pillow-wise than a sofa with color.

Neutral Is Less Expensive

Now this something you probably won't hear anywhere else. I remember so many articles I have read over the years about decorators or designers who had a neutral home. They said they were bombarded by colors all day long, and so they wanted soothing neutrals when they got home. Well maybe, but I suspect there is more to the story. The thing is, neutral is always in style. When you spend a lot of money on your furnishings (or even if you don't), you don't want to replace them every few years. For designers, decorators, and design bloggers, it's important that their homes are always in style. So if you want to be in style all of the time without having to replace things constantly, then neutral is the way to go. It may not be the current trend all of the time, but it never goes out of style.

If you are thinking you want to change things up, but you can't because your home is full of color, that is exactly what I thought. It was not easy for me to convert my home to neutrals, but I did it. I was able to keep costs down, since I did all of my own sewing—I simply slip covered my red furniture and made new bedding. It did require a good bit of my time, but I am SOOOO glad I did. So you pay one way or the other when you change your color scheme. I am one who thought I would never, ever be able to live with neutrals, and now most of my rooms are neutral. I love the soothing nature of white, cream, gray, and oatmeal. If you have a neutral home, or are considering going in that direction, I suggest that you not remove all color from the room. It will feel bland and flat with no color. Add a touch of color with some pillows, throws, a rug, artwork, flowers, or other accessories. I know after I spent months removing color from a room, it felt like I was going backwards putting color back in the room, but a bit of color is needed. The good news is that pillows or throws can easily be changed when you get bored with them. Better yet, if your whole house is neutral, simply move the accents around to different rooms for an entirely new look.

CHAPTER 17: BATHROOMS AND OTHER UTILITARIAN ROOMS

Bathrooms, also called "necessary rooms" are often overlooked when decorating a house. These rooms are usually small, and people sometimes have a difficult time finding a way to make them feel special. When I was a kid, a well-decorated bathroom was one that had a matching toilet seat cover, u-shaped rug (around the toilet), and towels. If you had all of these, you had a very hip, modern, "groovy" bathroom. Now things are so different, and there are so many very elegant upscale bathrooms. You can't just slap a towel and a candle in your bathroom and call it good now.

So how can you add style to a bathroom and give it a French flair at the same time? Here are a few suggestions.

Easy Tips for Redoing Your Bathroom

$ Ideas

1. Add a rub rack caddy to hold a book, soap, and washcloths.

2. Use a big jar to hold bath salts.

3. Use a vintage tea cup as a scoop for bath salts.

4. Roll up towels and keep them in a basket or crate.

5. Keep a fresh stack of clean towels sitting out for use.

6. Store extra toilet paper in a basket, crate, or bucket.

7. Store electronics out of sight.

8. Fill a cup with dried lavender or potpourri.

9. Add decorative hooks for robes.

10. Set out a pretty dish of French soaps.

11. Set out pretty towels.

$$ Ideas

12. Move a chair into the bathroom, if space permits.

13. Add a little table by the tub to hold a hand towel and soaps.

14. Use a small bookcase to hold towels.

15. Add a lamp.

16. Add an ottoman for extra seating.

17. Add a towel bar for wet towels.

18. Use a decorative rug rather than a typical bath mat.

19. Replace the old-style frameless mirrors with new decorative mirrors.

20. Change out shower curtain for a new one.

21. Remove dated cabinet doors and replace them with a curtain.

22. Cover the washer and dryer with a curtain.

If you are going to go to the expense of changing out light fixtures or plumbing fixtures, I highly suggest you go to a showroom, or at least check out an online site like build.com. I have nothing against shopping at big builders' supply stores, but they will not have the selection that the online and specialty stores will have. I want you to see all of your options before you decide. Look online to see what options are available there. I also think it is worth a trip to a local showroom that sells the items you need, be it lighting, plumbing, or something else. After you have done some serious looking, buy what appeals to you.

If what you saw at the big builders' supply store is what you want, now you can buy it with confidence. It pays to do your research before you install anything in your home. Even if the item isn't expensive, if you have to pay a plumber or electrician to install or remove it, you want to minimize those labor charges. Make sure the item you have selected is the design you like best, but also do some checking to see what kind of reviews the product has. Just because an item is expensive doesn't mean it will be reliable and well-made. Sometimes homeowners select very expensive faucets or light fixtures that break in a short period of time. With all of the online reviews, it is easy to find out whether an item is recommended or not. Just remember high price doesn't always translate into high quality.

$$$ Ideas

23. Use furniture for storage instead of cabinets.

24. Add electrical outlets for hair dryers and tooth brushes inside cabinets.

25. Update faucets.

26. Update counter tops.

27. Add a chandelier.

28. Update sinks.

29. Update lighting.

30. Add ceiling tile to the bath ceiling.

Some people feel their bathroom is too small to decorate, but that just isn't true. I agree that a small space means you will have fewer options, but you still have something to work with. You can usually add attractive storage space on a wall with shelving or hooks. Outdated mirrors and lighting can usually be changed out for better aesthetic.

City Bathroom

Curvy French mirrors accent this white bath.

Our builder suggested we put a little coffee bar in our bathroom, since that is a popular accoutrement for new homes in our area. I told him to leave the space open instead so that we could put our armoire in the space. The armoire holds towels, washcloths, sheets, and even extra pillows. I only store things inside that are white. Colorful quilts and blankets go in the armoire in my bedroom. Things automatically look coordinated if they are all the same color, and that is why I organize towels and blankets by color.

Setting a chair and table by the tub is nice if you have room. The table can be used to hold towels and soaps, while the chair can be used when you are changing clothes.

It's so easy to add some little accents without going overboard. This bath includes a vintage oyster basket full of rolled up luxury towels. A soft welcoming robe sits on the chair at the ready.

On the other side of the bathroom, we used curvy French mirrors to give the room a Frenchy feel. I found them at Hobby Lobby, then transformed them with paint and wax. The architectural prints on the wall showcase the buildings at Versailles. I chose not to use upper cabinets for a more open look. The light sconces also are very French in appearance.

The two tall pullout drawers house the hair dryers and toothbrushes. Our electrician set them up so that there is a power outlet in each drawer. Electric toothbrushes can be charged without being seen.

To give the room a spa-like feel, I added white plush robes to the room and hung them on some very adorable little Scottie dog

robe hooks. Since we are just talking about one or two hooks for robes, why not use a special hook rather than the plain vanilla ones?

Girls' Bathroom

The bathroom down the hall is much smaller. Here I used individual mirrors again above each sink rather than one big mirror. The light fixtures had a curvy feminine feel to them that felt French to me, same story with the curvy mirrors. They may not be French, but if they are curvy, they will probably go with a French look. Because there was unused space between the mirrors, I added artwork on the wall.

Downstairs Bath

This bath was lots of fun to design. I didn't want a traditional cabinet below the sink. I wanted something a bit more like furniture. I asked the carpenter to make the vanity like a little table. We used a marble bowl sink on top of the vanity, and used a wall faucet rather than the kind that connects to the vanity. The white granite on the vanity goes up the wall in an arched shape. I painted the vanity and distressed it using a technique very similar to the one I cover in the chapter on painted furniture.

Underneath the vanity, we used an antique oyster basket from France to hold rolled white towels.

The wall sconce was meant to be used in a foyer, but I was able to fit it in above the mirror. The gray painted metal sconce has lots of French detail.

The rest of the room was just as fun to plan. I added an old antique mirror above the sink. For a cornice board over the tub, I used a piece of salvaged barn wood.

The barn wood is worn in a way that you just can't replicate with new wood. Then I added the lace panels. Since this tub isn't currently being used, lace panels worked fine. If you want to use lace panels, or any other drapes as a shower curtain, be sure to add a shower curtain liner to keep the water inside the tub.

This little bath is more contemporary with its tilt mirror and quartzite countertop. The light fixture and the towel rack add a more flea market feel to the room.

Bev's Guest Cottage Bath

This bathroom below is very rustic. It certainly isn't considered traditional French style. When people think French, they think elegant, refined, and upscale. But I love to see French touches in all types of décor and find that it is just as much at home with rustic farmhouse style as it is with high-end contemporary design. I love the mix of rustic with refined. It reminds me of Green Acres, and Lisa Douglas was the one who originally came up with the shabby but elegant look. At the end of the day, the rest of us are just copying her style.

This is room has what I would call a "hint" of French. The artwork, the chandelier, and the curved mirror could be considered French. It is not a traditional French look as I said. But we are bending the rules to make French work in the modern home. We are breaking old rules, and I like that.

Luxury Farm Bath

The next bathroom is so fun and also has a hint of French. The silver, the wire shelf, the marble are some of my favorite elements, but my favorite is the mannequin head. Of course she has a tiara!

This owner chose to leave her windows uncovered, a bold move for a bathroom. It opened up the views to the outdoors. The wire shelf, the silver, tiara, and clawfoot tub add so many layers of details here.

Leslie's Bathroom

The soft blue of this bathroom is so refreshing. I love the way the light comes inside. A clawfoot tub completes the look. The little cabinet between the sink holds towels and a mirror.

Round Top Guest Bath

A more rustic approach, this bath uses a sliding old barn door at the entrance to the room. Inside the shiplap walls give the bathroom oodles of charm. Using a vintage mirror and wall cabinet also add so much interest and texture to the room.

The antique tin tiles on the ceiling complete the look. This room has so much to love from the floor all the way to the ceiling, and the truth is that it is a very small bath. I only point that out to say you can pack a lot of charm and detail into a small space.

Marble countertops make for a soft, pretty look.

Round Top Master Bath

Another rustic bath (left). This one has a bead board ceiling, and shiplap walls. The open cabinet stores bath supplies and towels. The small French table provides a place for towels or toiletries, while the chair is a great place to sit while changing clothes or putting on shoes.

Pair of English Cottage Baths

The double-sided slipper tub fits snuggly in this small bathroom packed with charm. The stone wall and beams give it a cottage feel. I like the brick floor and stone wall. It's a nice departure from an

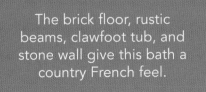

The brick floor, rustic beams, clawfoot tub, and stone wall give this bath a country French feel.

all-white bathroom. The second English bath includes a charming claw foot tub with a charming, old-fashioned ceiling mount shower rod.

Elegant Master Bath

This amazing bathroom reminds me of a ship's cabinetry. The arched top is just stunning. The marble wall behind the mirrors adds beautiful detail to the room. A tub sits on the other side with lots of detailed cabinetry and stylish windows.

Closets

If you have a small closet, like I had for most of my life, then there aren't a lot of things you can do to decorate it, but there are a few things you can do to make it the best it can be.

1. Color-code your clothes

    Not only does this make your closet look neater, it is a whole lot easier to find what you are looking for. I also organized my clothes by long sleeve, short sleeve, shorts, pants, and dresses. The organization makes it easier to find what I am looking for and also a pleasure to walk into my closet.

2. Use storage boxes for organization.

    The other thing you can do is use pretty boxes or baskets to organize and corral small objects in the closet.

3. Pick up clutter off the floor.

4. Add a chair or table if room allows.

5. Get rid of clothes you don't actually wear.

Even though my current closet is large, I didn't want it to become a junk shop. So rather than store stuff in here that I am never going to use again, I started giving things away. It's very freeing and fun.

Since we had the home custom built, I got to work with the carpenter to design a wall of built in drawers and cabinets. We keep sweaters, socks, and sheets in the drawers. With such a large closet, I wanted to make use of the space in the center of the closet. I had never had so much room in a closet before. Rather than go with a built-in island, I decided to keep the middle of the closet open. If I put an island in the center of the room, then I would be stuck with it later, even if I changed my mind. Using furniture instead, I can always completely redo the room if I so choose. I still have the option of moving a chest in here if I decide I need more storage. Now there a desk and two chairs, but tomorrow, I could move that all out and put a simple a large ottoman in the center. It is much more flexible if you don't go with too many built-ins. I work with clients who are stumped by big built-in cabinets that have been installed in bedrooms. We usually rip them out. Few built-ins look as good as real furniture.

With the open space in my closet, I decided to create a little French hideaway. I started with French gray paint on the built-ins. Then I used an elegant chandelier in the center of the closet. If we are barely awake, and don't want a lot of light, we turn on the chandelier, which is fitted with 25-watt bulbs. If we need more light for checking color matches, we turn on the canned lights. All of the lights come on if we are trying to determine if a sock is navy or black.

In the center of the closet, I added a French table and two leather Louis XV chairs. I know this closet is a real luxury, and to have room for a table and two chairs is beyond what I ever thought we would have. To be honest, it's a bit tight, but I really like having the seating area. Even if your closet isn't this big, my hope is that you can discover some ideas for use in your space.

Laundry Room

Laundry rooms are also notoriously small, but still there is room to make them charming with some French accents. I added a candle chandelier to the ceiling. It is non-electric, and the beauty of the candle versions is that you can put them about anywhere, since they don't require electricity.

CHAPTER 18: DREAMY BEDROOMS

Making a Bedroom Cozy

Bedrooms are meant to be a place to recharge. They should be beautiful and cozy, a place that surrounds you with warmth and comfort. The bedroom is not only where you sleep, but also where you want to enjoy quiet and rest. The room should embrace, not shock; therefore, I don't like jarring things in the bedroom, but instead prefer soft, natural fabrics, and soothing vistas.

For my own room, I chose a very soft, neutral, and relaxing palette. When using muted colors in the room, it's important to include lots of textures and a hint of color. This bedroom includes texture from the bed linens, artwork, bamboo shades, wood light sconces, reclaimed hardwood floor, and the furniture.

Since the bed takes center stage, it's critical to the feel of the room. Be sure to select bedding that is soft and inviting. I had previously spent a small fortune on gorgeous red bedding that, although beautiful, was not going to work with my new neutral palette. I had to think long and hard about no longer using that bedding, since it was so expensive. In the end, I decided to keep it . . . in the closet . . . where no one could see it. If I ever want to use it again, the bedding is there, but in the meantime it's not holding me hostage to a "red" room.

The finance industry would call the red bedding "sunk costs." The cost was in the past, and there is no way you can get that money back. But that doesn't mean I can't change out the bedding. And I could sell the old bedding if I wanted to.

After deciding to move away from the red, I then searched for the bedding of my dreams. I couldn't find exactly was I was looking for, so I decided to sew it myself from oatmeal-colored Italian linen. Since my settee and ottoman were also red, I knew I would have to make slipcovers for them as well. Making the slipcovers was much less expensive than having them reupholstered, and it is completely reversible, should I ever decide to go back to the original red upholstery.

The duvet at the foot of the bed is an antique French bedspread carefully gathered around a feather duvet. I bought the delicate antique bedspread with a plan to convert it to a duvet cover, but as often happens with antique materials, I found I couldn't take a scissor to this antique French work of art.

The antique French pine armoire is topped with an equally old French laundry basket. Like many treasures, this large basket was found at the Round Top Antique Show. The basket adds texture and authenticity to the room.

The armoire, filled to the brim with stacks and stacks of family quilts and linens, reminds me of my grandmother's house. On cold evenings, we would wrap ourselves in layer upon layer of quilts made by aunts and grandmas.

I love adding vintage touches to a room, and family heirlooms hold special value to me. It was so much fun to display the wedding gown my mother-in-law wore on a warm Virginia day in 1946, soon after WWII ended. Draped over the top of our old armoire, this satin and tulle wedding gown looks like the bride could be popping in at any minute to finish preparations for her special day. Displaying family treasures, like this inherited family wedding dress, makes the space personal and meaningful to the owner. I loved the look so much that I added my own wedding gown to the mix.

I really appreciate the warm, weathered pine in this antique French armoire. New pine pieces simply don't have the patina you see in antique pine pieces.

This simple satin wedding dress, although quite modest, still has a row of beautiful satin-covered buttons on each sleeve, along with a simple tulle ruffle.

A great way to add interest to a room is to use things in a new or unusual way. The cabinet I use as a side table was once the top of a grandfather clock (shown on page 221). Adding the shelf inside meant I could display an assortment of antique and vintage dishes inside the cabinet.

When designing a room, I like to think outside of the box. I want to not only create something beautiful, but also something unique that you don't see every day. When I converted a mirrored armoire in another room to a china cupboard, I had to remove the wood panel behind the mirrored glass. That wood armoire door panel sat in my guest room for years waiting for just the right project. When I decided to hang a candle sconce in my bedroom, the idea emerged to use the old armoire door as a base for the candle sconce. The door acts as a frame for the sconce, giving it more presence in the room, and adding an additional element of surprise and elegance.

To create an authentic French feel to a room, I used objects with lots of age. Sometimes the patina is from a hundred years of wear, and sometimes it is simply a faux finish used on the piece. The chippy paint finish on the settee and the stacked tables is the "real McCoy." They are both quite old.

Using pieces that show their age adds depth and appeal to a room. Using only pristine, brand-new pieces can make a room feel stuffy and too perfect.

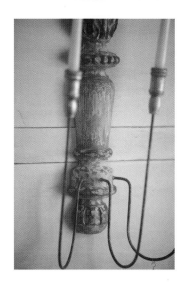

Although new, the sconces and lamps in the room appear to have an aged patina. I like to use a mix of new items along with antiques in the same room.

Linen is one of my most favorite fabrics to use when creating bed linens or slipcovers. Some people are put off by the abundances of wrinkles, but the wrinkles tell me the fabric is real linen. Nothing hangs like linen, and ruffles made in other fabrics just don't look like the same. It launders well, and because it is cool to the touch, linen is perfect for our hot, Texas climate.

When I found a French vanity at a nearby thrift store, it certainly didn't look like much. It was stained an unattractive orangey brown. I painted the vanity gray and distressed it to go with the antiques in the room.

The mirror over the vanity is a French Louis Felipe from before 1870. It was partially painted black when I bought it. I knew the black paint was not original, and it upset me greatly to see the mirror painted in that garish, morbid fashion. I painted over the black straight away because I couldn't stand it.

Later, when we traveled to Paris, I told my host, Madame Catherine, about how horrified I was to find my mirror painted black. Then she told me why it was black. She said that when Napoleon III lost the war in 1870, he lost part of France. The French people were so upset that they went into mourning. To show their collective grief, they painted much of their furniture and accessories black. That was an eye-opener. Lesson learned—Don't assume you know everything. (I'm talking to myself here!) I'm still not sorry I painted it, despite knowing that I painted over paint that had been added in 1870.

Evangeline's Room

Toile (pronounced twäl) is one of my very favorite fabrics. It says "French" like nothing else. This bedding was made in the same fashion as the bedding on my bed. Placing a quilt or duvet at the foot of the bed makes it even more inviting, even if the weather is warm. I used a pom pom quilt at the foot of the bed and vintage euro linen pillow shams. An easy way to add architectural interest to a room, is to add louvered doors behind the bed. I painted the doors, then distressed them using a antiquing glaze. An antique mirror hangs in the center of the doors, to give the room a bit of drama. If you use shutters or louvered doors behind your bed, you could easily eliminate the need for a headboard, but I already had one for the bed.

I used French chests on either side of the bed to act as night stands and storage for clothing. The antique table is used as a desk. I've covered it with a red striped grain sack. The wool-covered pouf makes a great place for putting your feet up.

Elise's Room

I love the rusty antique iron bed in the room below. I found it at a thrift store for next to nothing. It had just come into the store, and it immediately left in my car. The gray armoire hides a TV when it isn't in use. Whenever possible, I like to hide TVs and electronics from view. The bed, although not actually French, reminds me of simple country French décor. Not everything has to be French to appear French.

The owner of this lovely room enjoys sharing a snack with a friend while seated at the little table. From this upstairs bedroom, they can savor tea and scones as they watch birds playing in the pear tree out the window. Instead of artwork above the bed, I used an old mirror and two charming new sconces from Round Top. A room, much like a movie, tells a story, and it has a leading lady. For bedrooms, the leading lady is the bed, and what she wears needs to be consistent with the storyline. The storyline for a room is the feel you want to create. I wanted this bedroom to feel fun and fresh, while maintaining a rustic French charm. I pictured a simple, yet elegant bed much like you would find in the book *Madeleine*. I found this simple green striped long drop bedspread at Round Top. It is new, not vintage.

I always tell people I like "rusty, crusty, and chippy." This bed suits me to a rusty *T*. The rust finish on the bedframe just made my heart beat just a little bit faster. So the rust wouldn't ruin clothing or my delicate white bedding, I used a clear sealer all over the bed frame.

Although a bit unconventional, throughout the house, I used a darker gray on all of the doors. The doors become works of art, since they really stand out. The mahogany doors were custom made with French arches, pieced together the old-fashioned way. I used new crystal doorknobs in keeping with the old world feel of the home. As mentioned previously, I decided on new door hardware because I wanted the doorknobs to actually work, and I wanted door hardware throughout my home to match. If you decide on antique doorknobs, it's difficult to find enough matching hardware for an entire house, so one option is to just use it on a feature door, like a pantry.

In the city, I took a more formal approach to French design, but at the farm, I wanted a look compatible with relaxation and ease. The farmhouse is our get-away from a somewhat harried city life, so it was important that things remain casual, and they needed to stand up to heavier wear and tear.

The Three Little Bears' Room

I call this room at our farm "The Three Little Bears' Room." Both of my girls sleep in here, with an extra bed thrown in for a friend, since we often have guests at the farm.

The dresses on the walls are family pieces. One of the dresses was worn by both of my girls. The other dress and slip were purchased by my mother-in-law while she was expecting her first baby. Since that baby was a boy, and there never was a daughter, the dresses have never been worn, which explains their pristine condition. I love using the iron display boards, since I can take down the dresses if we ever tire of them, and change them out for something else. They also act as a frame for the dresses. Without these iron pieces, the small dresses would get lost on the large wall.

I have two sets of duvets for this room. Sometimes we use the watercolored floral duvets (Evie's favorite) and other times I use the lavender gingham duvets. It's fun to be able to change them out as the mood strikes us.

Cedar Hill Farm Bedroom

This bedroom is my happy place. Here I wanted something very simple and neutral, yet brimming with French charm. This long drop white linen bedding is so romantic. I've topped it with pale pink pillows and a duvet folded at the foot of the bed. The long blue velvet bolster gives the bed a distinctive look.

Simple leggy French chests on either side provide much needed storage in this small house, while the oyster baskets, below, neatly store magazines.

On the other side of the room sits an antique writing desk with a dreamy view down the pasture. It's a great place to work, where I can look out the window and daydream, when I should really be working. The desk is very old, from the 19th century. The antique French mirror above is full of character with the leaf and berry design.

Did I mention I love toile? Yes, I think I did. I added it to the back of my French linen press and to the inside of the doors. Adding fabric to the inside of furniture is an easy way to add some character to a piece of furniture. With this type of detail, it's tempting to leave the doors open all day long.

Guest Cottage

This is where guests stay at our house. The bedding is a mishmash of things. The cover is actually a bed skirt with a dainty lace edge. The quilt at the foot of the bed is a lavender and white toile. Next to the bed sits a vintage French bergere chair recovered in an oatmeal linen. There is also a dark plum velvet bolster pillow on the bed. I used a room divider next to the bed to give the room a bit of a paneled feel. To give it just the right amount of romance, I converted a canned light in the space so that we could install a chandelier there. The antique pine cabinet holds my fabric left over from many sewing projects.

This is also where I record my podcast, "Decorating Tips and Tricks." It is also hosted by Kelly Wilknisss of My Soulful Home and Yvonne of Stone Gable. This room is multifunctional and is also my sewing room.

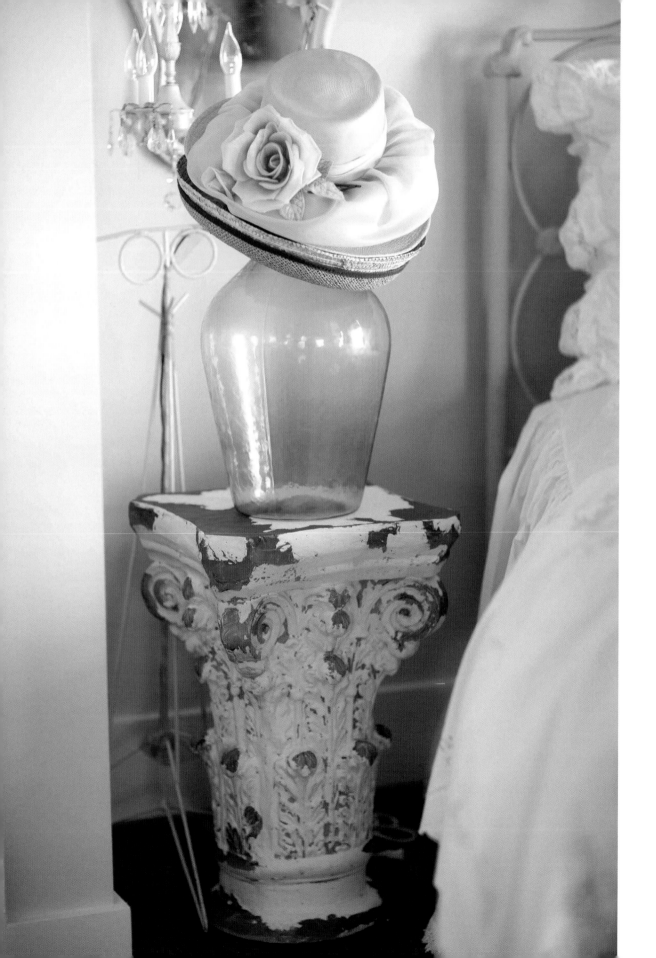

Texas Farmhouse Bedrooms

This blue and white bedroom is so full of peace and calm and still has lots of charm. The original oil painting above the bed, painted by a local artist, adds a pop of color and interest to the wall above the bed. The crisp white and blue bedding feels so inviting against the backdrop of the blue walls.

The guest room below boasts two twin beds right under a window upstairs at the farmhouse. This window looks out over the pasture where the horses graze. The soft blue and white embroidery on the bedding has a gentle beauty. Grandchildren make use of the room when they visit from the city.

The basket at the foot of the bed holds extra sheets and blankets.

Sears Kit House Bedroom

The room has a lovely vaulted ceiling with a round window above the bed. The floor is covered with a large gorgeous aubusson rug. The house was actually originally a made from a Sears kit.

Here you can see out the windows onto the pool and creek. The owner, Bev, has many collections and had a great eye for details. I could spend all day at her house and still find something new to see the next day.

A chandelier hangs down next to the bed for some bling and light.

Pool House

Bev has the most amazing pool house on her property. I have heard people say that city folk may collect cars, but country folk collect houses. There's a bit of truth in that. Bev has this incredibly adorable pool house. With the overhead doors open, it becomes an open-air kitchen and place to visit next to the pool. With the doors down, it's a little studio guest cottage with a charming kitchen, bath, and sleeping area.

The two daybeds in here can be used for seating or for sleeping. The concrete floor means there is no worry about spills on carpet or hardwood scratches.

I love the old stack of books and the antique bust.

Bev's creativity is amazing, as she used a basket around a chandelier in the corner. The walls are made from salvaged shiplap.

She has a vintage fan in the cottage, which comes in handy on hot summer days.

English Cottage Bedrooms

The stone walls in the cottage are the first things you notice. Although in Texas, this cottage was built to look like it stands in the English Cotswold's. English style furniture works beautifully with French furnishings, so this home is full of French touches. The mirror in the bedroom is curvy and beautiful. The dresser also has lots of details and curves.

The Swedish headboards are very charming with the two twin beds. Creamy matelassé bedding adds a flirty detail to the room.

The second bedroom at the English cottage also has

stone walls, which help insulate the home from the heat during the summer. Linen bedding adds a feeling of luxury to the room.

The bed is topped with vintage lace netting for a gorgeous effect.

A bedroom should be relaxing, and provide "a soft place to fall." While each bedroom highlighted here is different, they all share a common theme; they all have a touch of French flare, while providing a cozy

place to refresh and renew. A bedroom is the last place you see before you go to sleep, and the first place you see when you wake up. Shouldn't it be a special place that embraces you?

Round Top Blue Room

This room, tucked in the back of the house, has character to spare. The rustic fence acts as a headboard behind one of the beds. A mirror adds French flair to the room in an understated way. The blue toile quilts are just as charming as can be, paired with the long burlap bed skirts. Shiplap walls and bamboo window shades add texture to the room

Rustic Bedroom

This bed uses a reclaimed shelf as a headboard. Above the shelf sits a long mirror perfect for the space. A hand painted cube acts as a nightstand. The crown candle sconces proved the perfect touch of bling to the room. Mismatched lamps work beautifully on either side of the bed, since they both hold their own. The burlap bench provides a nice place to sit while getting dressed in the morning.

Guest Cottage

This adorable guest cottage provides so much charm, guests will have a hard time leaving. A converted crib acts as a settee in the room. Soft lavender duvets cover each of the twin beds that flank a small French hutch. The mirror is another French beauty.

CHAPTER 19: OUTDOOR LIVING

Making Outdoor Spaces Inviting

Our house sits in the middle of neighborhood founded in the late 1800s. At that time, with no air-conditioning, people spent a lot of time outdoors enjoying a cool breeze or any air movement they could catch in the summer. Porches were a vital part of the home. This was a time when a porch was used for sleeping in the summer, since bedrooms were often too hot. Neighbors spent a good bit of time on their porches not only trying to find respite from the oppressive heat, but also as a form of socializing.

Before computers, TV, and social media, the way most people related was in person, and that was what the front porch was for—visiting. A visitor would be offered a seat and a cold glass of iced tea. Neighbors might be strolling by, and they would be hailed and often invited over for a visit. This is the atmosphere I like to recreate on my porches. I love that neighbors are constantly walking by my house. It's a very walkable neighborhood.

Really one of the biggest tips I can give you about making our outdoor rooms livable is to treat them, as much as possible, like an indoor space and decorate them like you would an indoor space. Of course, you'll need to make some adjustments for the elements, which I discuss in the next section.

So what can you do to make your porch, deck, patio, or other outdoor area inviting?

1. Comfortable seating (obviously the bigger the porch the more seating you will be able to have)

2. Pillows

3. Blankets, quilts, throws in cooler weather

4. Side tables (if you have room)

5. Dining table (if you have room)

6. Indoor/outdoor rug

7. Rockers

8. Porch swing

I even have two daybeds outdoors. Stuffed with lots of pillows, they work beautifully as sofas, but remove the pillows, and you have a comfortable place to take a nap and feel the breeze. I just love having as many places as possible to sit and visit with friends and family.

Protection from the Elements

There is a secret to keeping indoor fabrics nice when they are in use on an outdoor porch. You don't want them to get wet or get too much exposure to the sun. Critters can also be an issue. My advice is to bring in the pillows and seat cushions when not in use. I know this is not what you want to hear, but it's true. I've tried leaving cushions and pillows outdoors at the farm. The fabrics were outdoor fabrics made to stand up to the elements, but the mice destroyed them.

Candles left outdoors were dragged behind furniture and gnawed—mercilessly. But that's at the farm. The cushions at my city house fare much better. I don't have a problem with mice in the city, but the squirrels have really torn up some cushions on my front porch. Then there's the cat who thinks our front porch is his, but otherwise he's pretty harmless.

The bedding on my back porch and at our treehouse go indoors at night. So far, almost everything has survived. I've had one table get ruined when it got too wet, but everything else has done well. The other thing I do is tarp my wood tables when the weather is foul or when we aren't there. I paint the iron furniture once a year. Keeping things outdoors means they will require a lot more maintenance.

I recommend checking what the manufacturer suggests, although I have dragged a china cabinet, daybed, and a few tables onto my porch that were meant for indoor use only. Things get dirty in the country, so I am also always wiping things down. It's a lot of work. But having said that, I feel it is well worth the effort.

Idyllic Outdoor Dining

When I think of French dining, my thoughts go to our experiences dining at outdoor tables along sidewalks in Paris. These trips to France were halcyon days. Having read many a décor magazine (like a teenager eagerly soaking up a gossip magazine) I had read about many a family meal at a long table beside a shabby, but elegant country home in the south of France. The wood table having been pulled out of the house earlier that day along with odd chairs, would be set up elegantly using family linens, country crockery, and real silverware. There were no plastic sporks to be found, no processed foods, paper plates, or paper napkins. These affairs were considered rustic by French standards, but were still incredibly elegant. That is the look I strive for . . . a look that says, "Welcome, I'm glad you are here!" I want my guests to know they are special and that I went to a little extra

effort to make our meal an event.

I don't use my "best china" outdoors, but I do use real dishes. When taking a picnic basket to our Creekside deck, I often grab some enamelware plates and mugs, so I don't have to worry about breakage. Still, I like the feel of the enamelware dishes better than paper plates.

My family loves taking a meal outdoors. Even a cup of tea or coffee in the morning outdoors is enough to make me smile.

My Back Porch

The daybed on our back porch makes the space so inviting. People don't often put a bed on the porch these days, but before air-conditioning, it was not unusual for families to sleep on the porch. I love taking a nap on the porch.

My favorite place to enjoy a meal with friends is at the long antique scrubbed pine farm table on our back porch. From the table you can see hay bales, trees down the hill, and the sun setting in the evening. The china cabinet is next to the table on my back porch. Well, why not?

Bev's Porch

My friend Bev has an amazing home with lots of fabulous porches, so she could quite easily live on her porch if she had to. She used an antique baby buggy frame, and added a board to create a unique coffee table.

Having a wonderful table on the porch means you can dine in style outside. It's like a picnic, but with more comfortable seating, close to a stove and refrigerator. It means you can use real dishes.

I love using real dishes outdoors. Yes, every time you use a plate, you run the risk of breaking it, but what is the point of having something that doesn't get used?

The head vase is an original. These vases were quite popular in the '30s and '40s. I remember my grandma had one.

A colorful vintage tablecloth, real dishes, and we are all set for a delightful meal. After the meal, we can visit on the other porch in wicker chairs as we catch the afternoon breeze.

I just don't think you can have too many places to sit outdoors. When you have company, you can spread out, and use several different seating areas.

Everything tastes better outside anyway, so why not dine al fresco?

The cupola adds a vintage feel to the outdoors. Although not French, with the curves and rusty metal, the cupola FEELS French, and that gives it lots and lots of appeal.

English Cottage Garden

Dinner for two at an iron bistro table in a manicured courtyard is so very French in my book. This enchanted garden makes for a luxurious place to linger over a meal.

The Fields

Even without a porch, it's simple to have an outdoor meal. You can easily set up a folding table, or even bring a table out of doors for an impromptu meal.

Everything tastes better outdoors anyway. Granddad always said that, and he was right. I've been known to carry chairs and a table out to the fields or even into the woods for a special meal. You can also haul a bed outside. (Yes, I've done that too.) But if that's too much work, a hammock might be just the thing for you.

Molly, our farm collie, loves to frolic in the wildflowers.

Tiny Chapel

This charming little chapel is a real favorite of my mine. I knew about the chapel long before I met Leslie, its charming owner. Taking our little all-terrain vehicle around the nearby dirt roads, we happened upon this chapel one day. I wanted to know more about it. It just had country charm. I knew there was a story there.

About a year later, when volunteering at VBS at our local church, I met the owner! Leslie, a delightful soul, had the chapel built before they even had a house on the property. It is built in a style similar to the way churches were built in this area when it was originally settled in the early 1800s.

You can see that the interior is authentic—so authentic, that there is no air conditioning or even electricity.

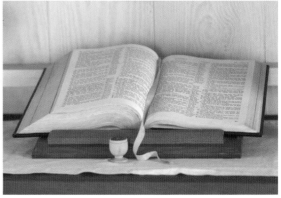

Cecile's House

Cecile's home is amazing, and her outdoor spaces are some of the best places to sit outside and enjoy the views. She has a side porch where we can see the sun set.

The front of the house provides yet another spot to sit a spell, with chairs, a bench, and even a porch swing.

Catch a breeze on the quaint front porch.

CHAPTER 20: BEFORE, DURING, AND AFTER

It's one thing to show pictures of a decorated room, but how do you do it? What is the thought process? How do you decide what to keep, what get rid of, and what to buy? I want to share with you my creative process. Here I'll show you my process start to finish, the decisions I made, and the end result.

Farm Master Bedroom

PHASE I

I'll show you the process I went through to transform my farmhouse bedroom from cottage style to Farmhouse French style.

From looking at the photos and my own tour of the room, I made some quick notes about the room:

- **Paint:** Although I would prefer a gray color on the walls, the current color is quite acceptable to me (Sherwin Williams Windsor Greige) so I am not repainting the room. I would prefer a shade more toward gray, but since the color is fine, this is an expense that isn't worth it for me.

- **Rug:** It's a green wool rug I got for $25. Although it went with the original green bedspread, I am no longer using that bedspread, and this rug does not have a French feel. It needs to go! Replace with neutral rug.

- I don't care for the green bedding. I want a cleaner look.

Before

- The painting is not the look I am going for in this room.

- Lamps on nightstands not working; they are too skinny; need something more bulky to go with the King bed.

- Nightstands, keep.

- Wicker chair looks too casual; the other chair not comfortable; they have to go.

- Stacked footstools between chairs—cute but not French; move them out.

- Chair at desk—don't like for this room.

- The painting above the desk is green and yellow and is not going to work well with my new blue-and-white room.

- Green ladder on wall may be too casual. I might need to move that depending on what I do here.

- French linen press works great, leave it.

- Antique desk is great, leave it.

So I have a list of things I now need for the room.

Buying List:

1. Neutral rug

2. Two comfy French chairs

3. Little side table for between two French chairs

4. Two new lamps for the night stands

5. New bedding

6. New artwork above bed

7. New artwork above desk

8. New desk chair

Now some rooms need just a few things; I would call this a pretty substantial list of things to replace. If on a budget, it may take months to replace everything, or maybe just a few days, if you can move items in from another room. Not everything has to be bought at once. Now I have a starting point.

For this room, I now have a buying list. Next, you're going to watch my buying process in action. I'll tell you how I selected new Items and where I bought them. I'm also listing the items in order, so you can see which purchases triggered other changes.

Bedding

PHASE II

When I am decorating a bedroom, it is difficult to find bedding that is just right for the room. I like to select the bedding first before I select any other fabrics for the room.

This gorgeous French blue ticking duvet and pillows came courtesy of Ballard Designs. I chose this bedding, because it is simple, yet elegant, causal, yet full of style. The blue stripe gives it a French feel, so I felt like this was the prefect bedding for my room. I am also in a "blue" mood so I knew the bedding was simple, yet classy, but it was also a color that I wanted to use.

PHASE III

Later, I decided I really wanted a long drop bedspread in the bedroom. I chose a white gauzy linen bedspread from Bella Notte. It has matching white linen ruffled euro shams. To add some color, I added the pink Shabby Chic pillow shams and pink duvet at the foot of the bed. The long blue velvet bolster pillow is what sets this room apart. Having a wow piece is so worth it in a room. A regular bolster pillow would have been lovely, but going with this large size in the sumptuous velvet elevates the bed to new levels.

Neutral Rug

PHASE II

I tried removing the green rug and going with no rug. It was an improvement, but I missed having a rug in the room.

PHASE III

We opted for a piece of carpet custom cut for the room. I wanted the wood floors to show through, but we also

Phase I

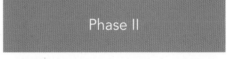
Phase II

Phase III

wanted a rug for cold nights. It's visually appealing to have one large rug that goes under the bed. It might feel like you are paying for a large part of the rug that you can't actually use and you would be right, but visually, it's very appealing. This rug is also quite neutral. It has a tone on tone pattern.

Pair of Comfy French Chairs

PHASE II

Now people ask me all of the time where I get my chairs, and why I chose the ones I did. As for these chairs, it was all dependent on what was available at my resale shops within my budget. I never know what is going to be available, since it is all second hand, and therefore what is in the store one day will be quite different from what is available another day in another

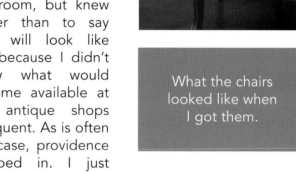

month. I wanted two nice French chairs in the room, but knew better than to say they will look like "x" because I didn't know what would become available at the antique shops I frequent. As is often the case, providence stepped in. I just happened to be at a

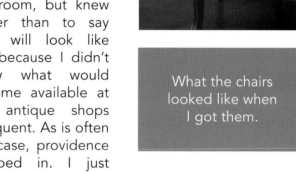

What the chairs looked like when I got them.

local consignment store, and saw two chairs covered in rust-colored fabric.

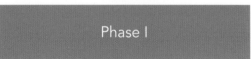

Phase I

Phase II

They looked pretty bad; in fact, someone had already started pulling the old fabric off the chairs, but didn't finish. I bought them quickly! They were a pretty decent price. I don't have a lot of room for chairs in this space, but these bergere chairs are small, and I knew they would work perfectly. I recovered them in vintage grain sack fabric for the backs, and a matching oatmeal-colored linen for the seats. Even when you consider my total cost (the chairs + fabric + labor), they were about half of what I would have paid for them, had I found them already recovered in linen and grain sack fabric. For the best deals you will need to go often to your favorite resale shops and check the stock. If they get what you want in the store, you need to move quickly and buy it before someone else does. Don't stop to think about it, or wait for the price to go down. Finding new chairs was certainly an option, but they would not have all of the marvelous hand carving on them, like these chairs do. When looking at old chairs, make sure to factor in the cost of fabric and the upholstery labor. It is typically cheaper to buy vintage chairs and pay for the upholstery work rather than to find them already reupholstered. I went with vintage chairs not to save money, but because I wanted those beautiful carved details.

Had these chairs not been available, I would have considered some other options. I would have used only one chair if necessary, but I did hope for a matching pair. I chose the grain sack and linen fabric because they are fabrics I love to work with, and I already had them in my work room. I also knew the grain sack stripe would be fabulous with my new blue bedding.

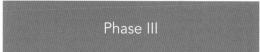
Phase III

PHASE III

I kept the French chairs, but changed out the pillows for these cheery lavender pillows.

Little Side Table

PHASE II

I knew that the chairs I was adding were much more upscale than the old chairs. The stacked step stools I had used in my previous bedroom design were not going to work with my new chairs. I also needed something very small for my space. I didn't want a table that was too tall, because I thought it would look odd next to the chairs. I thought of using a round side table, but the tall ones looked like plant stands. It needed to be the correct height for my chairs. Since I shop at secondhand stores, I never know what stock will be available at any one day.

I looked at new tables and old tables. I wanted something unique, but again it had to be small. That eliminated most of the tables. Then I saw this very short little white French table at Heights Antiques on

Yale. Originally it was probably a little telephone table or a nightstand. Although there were two, I just needed one. It was already painted; I used it just the way it was.

PHASE III

I added a gorgeous French candlestick lamp to the table for reading.

Pair of Lamps

As I like to say, I'm never done decorating. I rotate things until I get just the right piece in a room. I've tried five different sets of lamps here, until I found the perfect set.

Lamp shade too skinny.

Lamp too skinny.

Lamp too dark.

Lamp too fat.

Lamp just right.

New Artwork above Bed

PHASE II

As the bedding has changed, so too has the artwork. When I changed the bedding out, it was time to move away from the yellow artwork in this room. It's not just about assembling things you love, but selecting things that work together. I felt the artwork just wouldn't work with the new look. I wanted something big and more neutral for wall above the bed. The room has nine-foot ceilings, and with a king-size bed, I felt it needed something BIG. I tried several looks (you can see all of those in chapter three). In the end, I went with a large French mirror and the ironstone platters. It is simple and provides a focal point

PHASE III

For phase III I've kept the French Trumeau mirror and the white platters.

After Purchase #5: Small mirror on wall.

Phase I

Phase II

New Artwork or Mirror above the Desk

PHASE II

I wasn't sure what I would find for the space above the desk, I just knew the colors in the old painting weren't working with the blue and white. This is a problem that wasn't as obvious until I photographed the room. The chairs, and the bed looked like they were belonged in a blue room, while the other side of the room looked like it belonged in a green and yellow room. I decided to move the large painting out and replace it with something else.

Phase I

Phase II

As I was strolling through Chippendale Antiques in Houston, I found a lovely French mirror. The shop owner thought it was about a hundred years old. After inspecting it, I suspect she is right.

I felt that the three chairs were crowding the space too much, so I chose to use just one. Switching to just one chair, changing out the busy artwork for one mirror, and simplifying what was on the desk made for a cleaner look.

PHASE III

I felt the room lacked color, so I moved the mirror to a new home and added the arched religious art to this wall.

Phase III

New Desk

PHASE II

I kept the same desk from Phase I.

PHASE III

I wasn't looking for a new desk, but wasn't in love with the old one. Then on a fortuitous trip to Round Top, I found this amazing gem at the Compound. It came with a matching (expensive) chair I did not need. I asked the seller to just sell the desk to me, and was told no. Later when someone wanted to just buy the chair, my wish was granted and this Parisian number came home with me.

New Desk Chair

PHASE II

The original chairs were not French. I had an extra French chair sitting around (imagine that) so I moved it in here. It's an antique, I suspect, from the 1800's. It has a bit of damage, but nothing that would keep me from using it. (See page 256.) I've had this chair for about twenty years, so it has been in a variety of rooms. Because I really love the chair, and it is small, I have been able to use it in many different rooms. Sometimes we buy something we aren't so crazy about just because we need a particular piece of furniture right away, or it was the right price. That is the type of furniture we end up not keeping. Try to only buy things you love. When you see something that makes your heart sing, that is the piece. Then when you dearly love the furniture, you will find a place for it, when you redecorate your home.

PHASE III

I decided a gray French chair would work best with the new gray desk. I love the new look.

Linen Press

PHASE II

I wasn't unhappy with the styling of the linen press. Just thought I would change things up a bit. I get tired of a look after a while, so it's nice to move things around. I didn't buy anything new; I just pulled things from other places. The added basket and enamel bowl are both vintage.

PHASE III

I wanted a simpler look, so I removed everything and replaced it with one basket on top of the linen press. It's a very simple change, but I really like the look of just one big basket there. As we say on our podcast "Decorating Tips and Tricks," bigger is better and less is more.

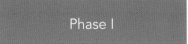
Phase I

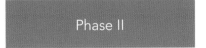
Phase II

Phase III

Phase I before with red, hand-painted chest and red rug.

Girls' Bedroom

Here is another example of what I did to give a room French accents.

The girls' room at the farm had a bit of French flair. The beds, if not Frenchy, were certainly French-ish. I define French-ish as maybe not French, but as something that is curvy, delicate, and feminine. The beds are definitely French-ish.

From my initial assessment, I was unhappy with the red rug. Although I did pick out the rug, and I love flat weave rugs, I decided the rug wasn't going to work with the new direction I was taking the room. I wanted the room to look a bit more French and not as red. I wanted to get rid of the red dresser and the red rug. I wanted to move the farm chair out of the room also. The lamps on the dresser, I just didn't like any more. I originally bought them to go in the blue room shown above, because they were green and went with my green pallet. When I changed colors, I didn't like the lamps so they went. Had I adored the lamps, I would have found a place for them somewhere. The antique French nightstands were, of course, staying.

1. I was removing the dresser because it was too red and it didn't work in the direction I was going.

2. The chair was to be removed because it was not French, and it was pretty wobbly.

3. The rug I wanted to get rid of because it was too red and seemed to clash with my new direction.

4. The dresser lamps I didn't like any more. I wasn't that crazy about them, when I bought them. Lesson learned.

5. The mirror was also going. I liked it but didn't think it would go with a new French dresser.

So that is the list of things I didn't want in the room any more, and why I didn't want them. To give a room French accents, you do NOT need to get rid of everything that isn't French. I was tired of many things in this room, and was as good a time as any to get rid of them.

Beds

PHASE II

I know this may sound crazy, but even as I was removing red rug and dresser) I was simultaneously adding a touch of pink. Well, the beds felt too bland all white, so I decided I would add pink throws at the end of each bed with some color. I didn't want too much color, just a hint. I looked all over and just couldn't find what I wanted.

To be completely transparent I didn't know what I would like so I tried a few different options. I wanted a bit of color back in the room, but not an over-

Phase I

Phase IIa

Phase IIb

Phase IIc

whelming amount. Some people said that my room without color looked like a hospital ward at Downton Abbey. Ha! I doubt that was meant as a compliment, still I thought, *Hey, it could be worse!*

Here I tried a few different looks, the white beds with no color, then I added an Ikea red and white duvet. I tried it covering the bed, then I tried folding it a few different ways. Next, I tried lavender gingham duvets. I want you to see that I tried several different looks to decide which would be best. Some designers buy several different items, then after trying out each one, they keep one option, and return the rest.

Phase III

PHASE III

I have used purple, blue, and pink watercolor bedding for Phase III. My daughters love the watercolor bedding so that is what is on the beds. I still love the lavender gingham bedding, so I can always go backwards any time I want.

| Phase I | Phase II and III |

Before and after with the brass lamp painted black.

Chest

PHASE II The old chest had color that was too strong. I also wanted an antique with graceful lines. The new chest, which isn't new at all, looks like it was made for the room. I found it at Heights Antiques on Yale. It was a beautiful chest with lots of details.

PHASE III I love the chest, so I kept it.

Lamp

PHASE II The old lamps I never did like. The new lamp was simply moved in from the master bedroom. I gave the white set of lamps away to someone who was happy to have them. I bought this lamp second hand. It was brass and had a dated shade at the time. I replaced the shade with a new linen drum shaped shade. I painted the brass lamp base with black paint to give it an updated look.

PHASE III The lamp still works, so we kept it.

Mirror

PHASE II The old one was not going to work with the antique chest. It doesn't look right with the French chest, so as soon as I found the chest, I knew that would have to be moved to another room. The new French mirror also adds presence to the room. It's very tall and has a soft French green color.

PHASE III I kept the mirror from phase II. It's perfect for the room.

Rugs

PHASE II I took out the large red rug. I still like it, just not in here. Rather than replace it with another large expensive wool rug, I found some small ones at TJ Maxx to go between the beds. They were much cheaper, and I didn't really need one big rug in here.

PHASE III Like in the master bedroom, we had a custom rug custom made for this room. It's tone on tone, about fourteen feet wide. I felt the burlap covered ottomans no longer went with the look in the room, so I changed them out for the lavender benches. The baskets fit neatly below for personal items.

Make Mistakes

One reason I wanted to include the process I used on these rooms is because I think sometimes people believe, incorrectly, that designers and decorators have some magic touch, and that they get it right all the time with no mistakes and no experimenting. That is simply not true. If this mythological creature exists, I would love to meet him or her. Decorating is trial and error, one step forward and two steps back, especially in the beginning. It's okay to make mistakes. That is part of the process. The point is to learn from your mistakes, and not hit yourself over the head. With each mistake, you are learning. Everyone has to start out as a beginner. **To be a good decorator you have to be willing to be a bad one first.**

If something doesn't work, then try something else. Try to figure out what about the room isn't working. That will help you determine what you should do to fix it. If you don't know which pillow is the best one for your room, buy five and try them all. Keep the one that works, and return the rest. The more you focus on your decorating skills, the more you will improve.

If you are stumped, ask for help. You can ask a friend who has a good eye, or hire a professional. Some stores will even help you for free. Read books on design, subscribe to design blogs, look at magazines. There are so many sources available. Save ideas on Pinterest.com or Houzz.com. Also, don't forget to photograph your room. Looking at those photos will be a very valuable exercise, even if you are the only one looking at them. Those photos will tell you what is working and not working.

So how did I know this would all work together? Well clearly I didn't, since I had to make a few adjustments to my original plan.

After I finish the room, I ask myself if it holds together. Does it look better than it did before? Does it excite me now, or does it feel ho-hum? I usually know when I see the photos if I am done or not. Of course, even when I am done, I'm never really "done."

Phase I

Phase II

Phase III

CHAPTER 21: PULLING IT ALL TOGETHER

Decorating is a process. Don't feel bad if you buy something and it doesn't work. This happens to talented designers and decorators all of the time. Sometimes you have a plan in your head, but it looks different when you put it all together. You will need to make some adjustments as you go. Even after I decorate a room, often it still needs something else. Sometimes a rug needs to be exchanged, or a something I ordered isn't the color I expected it to be. After I make all of the planned changes to a room, I step back and take a second look. I look at all of the changes along with what was already in the room. Does it all work together? Is it pleasing to the eye? Rarely does a plan come together without some tweaking. Let's say you did your analysis of the room, photographed it, put a shopping list and followed your plan to a T, and it still looks not quite right. Don't panic. Just step back and try to determine what isn't working. Take another photo and look at it again. Phone a friend. If you have a friend with a good eye, ask her (or him) what you should do. At the end of the day, it is your house, and you need to love the way it looks. All is not lost if you aren't happy with the room. It might only need some slight tweaking.

What Do You Do If Your Room Still Isn't Right?

Let's try our original exercise and see if we can get your room just the way you want it. This is just meant to be a tool to help you put a plan together for your house.

Go outside, and come in your home with fresh eyes. Pretend you are a visitor in your home. You can even bring a friend with you who will be honest with you.

Walk into the room and pretend like you have never seen it before.

1. What is the first thing you notice about the room?

2. What feeling does it evoke?

3. Does it feel warm and inviting?

4. Is this a room you enjoy being in?

5. Does it feel dated?

6.   What do you like about the room?

7.   What would you like to change about the room?

8.   Do you like the colors in the room?

9.   Does the room feel cluttered?

10. List the items you don't like in here.

11. List the things you do like in here.

12. Does the room flow, or does it feel choppy?

13. Does it feel balanced?

14. Do the colors and patterns work together or feel like they are fighting?

15. Is the furniture functional for the room?

Take some more photos and examine those again.

I am hopeful your home is getting closer to where you want it to be. If you are seeing improvement, then that is very exciting news, congratulations. It may take a while for you to get the room just like you want it. I have been tweaking my house for years. It's okay to try different things and move things around. Buy some new things, but keep the tags in case you want to return them. If you are still stuck, then seek some professional decorating advice. Even if you just hire someone for an hour or two consult, that will be well worth the money spent. An expert can often tell you things that might have taken you years to figure out on your own. We all get stuck in a rut, thinking things have to be arranged the way they are. New eyes, especially when they belong to someone talented, can provide some wonderful, fresh ideas.

If you use a professional for your consult, be sure to include your notes for the assessment above. Write down any specific questions you have for your decorator. Make good use of your time. Listen and try not to talk too much. You are usually paying per hour. Some decorators will even work with you online using your photos. They don't always need to come to your home.

So what if you realize now that you have made some decorating mistakes? Breathe! It's not the end of the world. I make mistakes all of the time. This is how we learn and grow. My motto is "If you aren't making mistakes, then you aren't learning anything." If you purchased something you dislike, hopefully it is returnable. If it isn't and you just can't stand it, then think about consigning to a consignment store or selling it on Craigslist or eBay. If you don't like a paint color you used on a chair, then maybe you can paint it again another color. It is helpful if you can limit your mistakes to small ticket items. Ovens and refrigerators are difficult to return, and expensive to replace.

Let's say you bought something you don't like and you don't have a place you can sell it. Do you have a friend that likes it? If so, can you do an exchange? There is usually a way to fix most anything. Sometimes you just need to be a bit creative. When I make a mistake, I try to figure out a way to fix it. Sometimes the fix is easy if it just requires a return. One time I started painting a wall. I hated the color. I wondered if I should stop. Then I looked at how many gallons of paint I just bought. I kept painting. I wondered if maybe it would look better when I finished the wall. It didn't. Then I thought maybe it would look better once the paint dried. It didn't. Note: As soon as you notice you don't like a shade of paint, STOP. Don't keep painting, thinking you will like it better later. I don't care how many gallons of paint you bought. Trust me; you will be sorry.

Sometimes I buy a chair and I don't end up liking it in the room I bought it for, but it works great in another one. Things get rotated a lot at our house. That's another reason to keep similar colors in several rooms, so you can move things around if you want to.

Decorating a home is not something you do once and you are done. Your home should evolve with you as your tastes change and grow. It's okay to mix things up, and change your home. Experiment and have fun.

CHAPTER 22: FINAL THOUGHTS

I'm going over all that I covered and thinking, *Did I forget something?* Did I leave something out? What do I really want you to remember? I know this is the last chapter, and this is my last chance to reveal decorating ideas. What are the things I really want you to remember? Here they are.

Create Your Own Style—Don't Follow the Fads

Your home should showcase your style, not the latest fad. Your home needs to embrace you, your family, and your friends. In my mind, it's not about showing off; it's about making your home special for you. I know some people make decorating a competitive sport, but please don't get caught up in that. It can be expensive in more ways than one. The competitiveness can make decorating stressful. If you are just redoing your home to impress others, then you may feel the need to change things out unnecessarily every year or two. If you select furniture that will impress, but it is not necessarily what you like, then you aren't going to be happy with it, and you will end up replacing it or detesting it. Decorating should be fun, not stressful. I don't suggest going with every fad, but it is wise to keep up with trends, meaning you should at least know what they are. You want to know what is in and what is out. Then keep that in mind when purchasing new things, especially big purchases. For example, you wouldn't want to buy a blue stove if they were on their way out, unless you really, really, really like blue stoves. That would be expensive to replace. But a blue pillow is typically not a big expense and could easily be replaced later when you tire of blue, or if it goes out of style.

Pace Yourself

Try to find things for your home that you LOVE, but you don't have to do it all in one day or even one month. I would rather have two things I am crazy about, then fifty ho hum things. Yes that's true. It's okay if it takes time to create the home you love. It probably will. The trap too many people fall into is buying something they can afford but don't like. Remember if you don't like it, I don't care what a great deal you got it for, you paid too much. Learn to embrace those empty spaces while you wait for that perfect something.

Step Out of Your Comfort Zone

I hope this book has encouraged you to try some new things, and maybe step out of your comfort zone. Getting a unique, beautiful look requires thoughtful reflection. I believe our homes affect our mood to a large degree. A beautiful, peaceful home is so important, especially as the world becomes a crazier place every day. Trust your instincts. Your style won't be the same as mine or anyone else's. You have your own unique look. Even if your look is still evolving, it is your look, and you have the final say on whether it works or not.

Sometimes clients have a piece I really don't like. I ask if they are open to moving or getting rid of it. If they say they want to keep it, I honor that because it is their house, not mine. Sometimes I do things in my home and the readers hate it. I usually consider their argument. Sometimes I end up agreeing and I make the change they are recommending. However, sometimes I just flat disagree. If I don't agree, then I do it the way I want to without apology. I have to live in this house. The homeowner gets the final say. Even if you disagree with your designer, the deal is if you don't like it, then it is wrong for your house.

They DO Notice

I have a story to share with you. My daughter has never had any interest in interior design; she loves music. That's fine with me. I want her to be who she is. I accepted the fact that she won't notice or appreciate what I do a long time ago. Then one day I asked her if she wanted a crystal lamp for her room. She was so excited and told me it made her room feel like "paradise!" It was a nice, and very unexpected, compliment. That goes to show that even if your family doesn't compliment you on your decorating skills, they still probably appreciate it.

Style Evolves over Time

Another thing I want to tell you is that it takes time for your style to evolve and emerge. Don't expect to knock it out of the ballpark your first time at bat. My first attempts at decorating were pretty embarrassing. Here's the thing about learning something new. You have to be willing to be bad at it in the beginning. Even if your first attempts aren't that great, don't give up. Failure is part of the learning process. Any forward movement is progress.

The Importance of Decorating

Some people see interior decorating as unimportant; I don't agree. Our homes are where we live out most of our lives. They will have an impact on the quality of our lives. The impact can be positive or negative. In the home we entertain our friends and family. I want those people in my home to feel welcome and loved. I hope that my home helps them to feel special. At the end of the day, a decorated home is all about how it makes people feel when they are there. It's not about having the nicest house on the block, or impressing visitors with how much money you have. I want them to feel inspired to create their own beautiful space. I want to create a welcoming environment where guests and family feel special and celebrated. If we can do that, then we have done something important.

Mother Teresa said, "We can do no great thing, only small things with great love."

FURNITURE & DECOR SOURCES

4   Chair from World Market, sconces and mirror from Heights Antiques on Yale in Houston, vanity from Junior Forum Resale shop, Houston

10   Antique pedestal from Old World Antiques, Round Top

13   KEW planter from Buchanan's Native Plants in Houston

15   Rug from Ballard Designs, antique desk from Morton Kuehnert Auctioneers

17   Brass tray from Soft Surroundings

18   Tall clock from Joss and Main, blue striped chair from Birch Lane, daybed from Restoration Hardware, lamp from Joss and Main, lavender pillow from BlueBellGray, ottoman from Aidan Gray

22   Gold-and-white tureen from Junior Forum Resale Shop, Houston

23   Crystal candelabra from Junior Forum Resale Shop, Houston

30   Slipcovered wingack chairs from Soft Surroundings, wall candle sconce from Aidan Gray

37   Canvas print from Joss and Main, turkish towel from Turkish T, oyster basket from Gallery Auctions, Houston

38   Brass tray from Soft Surroundings

39   Wood candlestick from Aidan Gray

41   Original oil paint - hay by Linsey Sappington, ceiling tiles by American Tin Ceilings, bedding by Ballard Designs

42   Table from Heights Antiques on Yale in Houston, pillows by BlueBellGray

45   Column table from Wisteria, room screen from Jubilee in Houston

47   Oeil de boeuf mirror from Restoration Hardware

48   Crystal chandelier from build.com

49   Small round and large bread board from Bill Moore Antiques, Round Top, large round bread board from Heritage Lace

51   Vintage lamp from Junior Forum Resale shop, Houston, Blue French shield from Antique Flea Finds (antiquefleafinds.com)

52   Lamps from Aidan Gray, pom pom quilt from Ballard Designs, chests from Soft Surroundings

55   Iron lamps from Heights Antiques on Yale in Houston

56   Chandelier from Horchow, lamps from Aidan Gray, table from Restoration Hardware, console from Restoration Hardware, rug from Dash and Albert, bench from Joss and Main, shades from Bali Blinds, curtains from Bali Blinds

57   Cherub from Wisteria, dried lavender wreath from Jackson and Perkins, blue velvet fabric from Calico

81   Church pew from Bill Moore Antiques in Round Top, ottoman from Aidan Gray, rug from Birch Lane

95   Bench from Junior Forum Resale Shop, Houston

101   Desk from Alisanne Wonderland in Round Top

102   Cupboard from Heights Antiques on Yale in Houston

103   Striped shower curtain from Pottery Barn

118   Bed from Charles P. Rogers, plaque above bed from Ballard Designs, lamps from Aidan Gray, bench from Aidan Gray

151   Dishes from Heritage Lace

153   Footed plate from Heritage Lace

155   Lace from Heritage Lace

174   Counter stools form Restoration Hardware, dishwasher from Thermador, chandeliers from build.com, refrigerator and freezer from Frigadaire

175   Gas range from Thermador, back splash tile from Walker Zanger

176   Fabric for chair from Calico, table from Restoration Hardware, rug from Dash and Albert, chair from Gallery Auctions in Houston

179   Armoire from Gallery Auctions in Houston, table from Gallery Auctions in Houston, side chair from Gallery Auctions in Houston, lantern from Ballard Designs, rush from Dash and Albert, shades from Bali Blinds

181   Tabletop throw from Turkish T, rug from Ballard Designs, table from Restoration Hardware, bench from Joss and Main

183   Chairs from Home Goods, table from Wisteria

190   Pedestal from Heights Antiques on Yale in Houton, chair from A&G Antiques in Houston

193   Rug from Ballard Designs, shades from Bali Blinds

196   Table from Wisteria, lamps from Aidan Gray

202   Doggie robe hooks form Anthropology

205   Purple towel from Turkish T, lamp from Target

214   Lamp from Aidan Gray, leather French chairs from A&G antiques in Houston, fabric for pillows from Calico

215   Washer and dryer from Samsung candle chandelier from Décor Steals

218   Bed from Charles P Rogers, rug from Rugs USA, bench from Aidan Gray

219   Wall candle sconce from Aidan Gray

220   Vanity from Junior Forum Resale Shop, Houston, curtains from Bali Blinds

221   French chair from Soft Surroundings

222   Bed from Charles P. Rogers, French chests from Soft Surroundings, lamps from Aidan Gray, French chair from Home Goods

223   Green striped bedding from French Laundry, iron bed from Junior Forum Resale shop, Houston, comfy chairs from Khols, shades from Bali Blinds, llinen curtains from Ballard Designs

224   Artwork from Joss and Main

225   Floral bedding from BlueBellGray, gingham bedding from Pottery Barn Kids

226   Long drop linen bedspread from Bella Notte

227   Bamboo rug from Décor Steals, room screen from Jubilee in Houston, chandelier on stand from Jubilee in Houston, pine cabinet from Heights Antiques on Yale

228   Large green bottle from Target, white column nightstand from Wisteria

255   Blue striped bedding from Ballard Designs, white long drop bedspread from Bella Notte, long velvet bolster pillow from Bella Notte, pink duvet and pillow from Shabby Chic

268   Postal scale from Bill Moore Antiques in Round Top

270   Tablecloth from Turkish T

273   Decorative pedestal from Heights Antiques on Yale in Houston

ABOUT THE AUTHOR

Anita says her ideal day is one spent on her back porch with friends and family around her large scrubbed pine table watching the sun set while enjoying a delicious meal. Her passion is interior design, and it has been her entire life. She chose a career in engineering only after her father insisted she would not be able to live off of an artist's meager earnings. And so for many years, she led a double life, wearing steel-toed shoes and a hard hat by day, then whipping up curtains and slipcovers by night. She kept her "decorating double life" a secret from her male colleagues throughout her corporate career.

In 1993, she and her husband welcomed their first child, Elise, who was born with Down Syndrome. Her second child, Evangeline, was born in 1996. Anita was a stay-at-home mom for many years while her children were young. As they got older, Anita was ready for a creative pursuit. She opened her own portrait photography business, and also developed an online photography course. Although she enjoyed her photography business, she was ready to return to her first love, interior decorating. Looking for a new challenge, she began working in a furniture and home décor shop, learning all she could about retail, furniture, antiques, styling, and marketing. After several years, she finally hit the publish button on her own blog, CEDAR HILL FARMHOUSE, in March 2011. She soon realized that blogging about interior decorating was a perfect fit for her.

It was slow going at first, but many years later, Anita's monthly reach across all channels is about six million. Her work has been featured in 20+ magazines, with five covers. Her blog was named one of the top country French blogs by Domino magazine, and Country French magazine named Anita one of their favorite stylemakers in 2016. She hosts the popular podcast DECORATING TIPS AND TRICKS with Kelly Wilkniss and Yvonne Pratt.

In July 2017, she was a winner of the first ever Dash and Albert rug design challenge. Her rug will be available for sale from Dash and Albert in 2018.